HOW TO DEVELOP A BETTER SPEAKING VOICE

HOW TO DEVELOP A BETTER SPEAKING VOICE

BY
MARJORIE HELLIER
(Formerly with The Old Vic. Theatre Co.)

Gold Medalist, London Academy of Music, A.T.C.L., L.G.S.M. Voice Specialist, The Abbey School For Speakers, Westminster, S.W.1.

Foreword by
ED PERRY
Hollywood Radio & Television
Announcer & Narrator

ILLUSTRATED BY THE AUTHOR

Published by
Melvin Powers
WILSHIRE BOOK COMPANY
12015 Sherman Road
No. Hollywood, California 91605
Telephone: (213) 875-1711 / (818) 983-1105

Copyright 1959

Printed by
HAL LEIGHTON PRINTING COMPANY
P.O. Box 3952
North Hollywood, California 91605
Telephone: (213) 983-1105

All Rights Reserved
Printed in United States of America
Library of Congress Catalog Card Number: 59-13321

ISBN 0-87980-056-9

FOREWORD

Have you ever heard your voice played back on a tape recorder? The first time you heard it, you probably said, "That's not me." The following thought was probably, "Do I sound like THAT when I talk?" And, the third silent thought was, "Better do something about it quick!"

But, what to do? How do you start improving your voice? The best solution is to take lessons from a voice teacher. This, however, costs money and takes time, both precious commodities. If your career is in the acting profession, this is the only solution. But, if you are not directly connected with the entertainment world, you will not want to go to such lengthy measures.

Having a good speaking voice is an asset in any profession, and nothing is more revealing about your personality than your voice. What does the voice do? It reveals all the emotions inherent in man —anger, frustration, happiness, contentment, etc. Actually, the impression you make on other people is not done with words, but how you speak them. The most important word in the human language today is "communication." Without it, enemies are made, friendships broken, business lost. When the phone was invented, the bulk of communications was taken from the hands and given to the voice. Yet, while children are taught their grammar and ABC's in school, the art of elocution is ignored.

Now, you have reached a point in your life when you realize something is missing, and, being a mature person, you naturally want to correct this lack. "Do it yourself" has become the national password, so your problem is finding a book that is easily understood, practical, and interesting. Look no further, you are holding it in your hands.

This book was written by a woman who has made her living by properly using her voice. Marjorie Hellier, actress, singer, lecturer and tutor with twenty-five years' experience in the handling of voices of every age and type, vividly describes her individual (and successful) approach to the art of voice control.

Marjorie Hellier has set down all the pertinent facts necessary for improving your voice, and has done it in such a delightful manner, you will find yourself eager to improve. With her simple instructions and illustrations, it will take only a short time for you to notice a remarkable change in the quality of your voice. If you don't believe it, go back to that revealing tape recorder after you have thoroughly digested and applied the principles taught in this book, and HEAR FOR YOURSELF.

Ed Perry

Hollywood, California

CONTENTS

CHAPTER	PAGE
PROLOGUE—THE MIRACLE OF SPEECH	11

Voice and communication. Two instruments in one. The Human Orchestra. We are practising all the time. What do *you* think? The privilege of speech.

1 VOICE AND HABIT 14

Your Natural Voice is perfect. Sounds and their association. Speech affects our thought. Hearing one's own Voice. Why make-do? Creative Mind and Habit Mind.

2 THE BREATH OF LIFE 22

Breath *is* Life. We taste, smell, think with our breath. It reflects every feeling. Breathing and Laughter. "Nerves". In-spiration—the physical facts. Unwanted breath. Deep breathing made easy.

3 OUR WIND INSTRUMENT 31

We are built for right breathing. Can you relax? Poise. Graceful carriage and good posture. Nose and Mouth Breathing. Some experiments. Feeble breath means feeble tone. The Universal Energy.

4 THE DOOR OF THE VOICE 41

The arch-enemy—Contracted Throat. Harnessing the yawn. Tongue-control. Whistling. Raise the roof! "AH Complex". Basic sounds of speech.

5 OUR STRING INSTRUMENT 49

What *is* Voice? Facts about vibration. Looking inside the voice-box. Four rules of sound. Tension and its problems. Effortless speech. Full breath harnessed to flowing tone and changing sound.

6 OUR NATURAL LOUD-SPEAKERS . . . 59

Resonance. The meaning of Echo. Our vocal arches. Acoustics. How physique affects voice. Rich tone versus loudness. Voice-power and will-power.

7 WAKING THE ECHOES 64

The Mouth Tunnel. Domes and Sounding boards. Humming. Nose and chest Amplifiers. Use all your breath on all your tone.

Contents

8 THE SHAPE OF WORDS TO COME . . 70
Many shapes and innumerable tones. Make the most of our good points. Equal distribution of labour. Lip drill. Whisper. "Oiling the hinges". Gape, pout and grin. Avoid mouthing.

9 SPEAKING AND LISTENING 77
Pronunciation. Standard English. Some common "lapses". The first letter of the Alphabet. Take pride in your Dialect. Long and short vowels. Yes and No. ER! The ill-treated *ow*. Normal versus affected speech.

10 MUMBLING—AND WHY 84
Lack of confidence. Thinking carelessly. Lack of ear. Ignorance. Quick thought and clear thought. Give your muscles time and room. A child's speech-toys. Early problems. Lisp.

11 OUR PERCUSSION INSTRUMENT . . . 90
Vitality of consonants. Five basic actions for lips, tongue and teeth. Sounds without voice. Twin-sounds. What the percussors do.

12 OUR NATIVE TONGUE 96
Does your tongue play tricks? Tip-training. Drooped words and fading sentences. Finish tells. Short-cut to clarity. Rebound. Slurring and telescoping. Tackle your weak spots. Word-collecting.

INTERLUDE—GETTING DOWN TO IT . . 103
How long will it take? Start on strangers. Dare to be different. Catalogue your Daily phrases. Common sayings of a common teacher.

13 CURES FOR MONOTONY 107
Everything changes, why not voice? Dead and alive speech. Tunes. Voice graphs. Hums and Grunts. OH. Alter your habit-rates. Flexible speech needs a flexible mind. Dead-pan faces. Eyes, Pause.

14 LIVING WORDS 114
Personality of words. Their structure and sound-value. Be word-conscious. Old sounds with a New Look. The thought behind the word.

15 VOICE AND VISION 118
The art of transmitting mind-pictures. Mind and Voice in sympathy. Sound-colours. Knowledge plus imagination. Your Voice reveals your heart.

Contents

FINALE—YOUR VOICE AND THE REAL YOU 121
You can do what you like with your own voice. Choosing your personality. Face up to your doubts. Your Voice *is* You.

Prologue

The Miracle of Speech

WHAT you *think* determines what you *are*. Your thoughts are the basis on which your personality is built. The influences that shape your thought—environment, upbringing, education, pastimes, companions—lie outside the scope of this book. It is with the *expressing* of your thoughts with which we are now concerned, and the expressing of them through the most vivid and direct of all channels available to *you*—Your Voice.

The voice as a means of communication is unique to human beings. We have other methods, in common with other living things; sound—as apart from speech—and movement: but these can only *suggest* what we wish to convey, whereas the voice expresses *exactly* what the mind dictates: or rather, is capable of doing so in exact proportion to our control of it.

The voice as a musical instrument is unique for the same reason, that it is able to transmit to its hearers the precise shade of thought and feeling, whereas in all other types of musical sound one can only guess at the message behind them, and this comes differently to every listener.

Another striking characteristic of the human voice is that it combines two instruments in one, or rather, it combines in one mechanism two distinct functions—Speech and Song. All speakers should be able to sing, and certainly all singers should be able to speak—by which I mean speak *well*. Both kinds of sound are produced by the same process in that they share the same source—the Voice Box, and the same motive power—the Breath; and they both come through the same hole. . . .

It seems strange that more singers have not tumbled to this fact—and taken advantage of it: their speech seldom has anything like the quality and control of their singing tone, yet

Release Your Voice and Find Your Personality

the two techniques are fundamentally one. (I still remember the shock at a concert, when a certain voluptuous-voiced contralto—applauded warmly for a glorious sacred solo—swept back to the platform and announced her encore in a breathy squeak.)

The two *arts* are very different, of course. The singer has to master tune, rhythm and long sustaining; the speaker has none of these problems to distract him, he is free of the limitations of notes and barlines. His choice of sound is quite literally "free as air"—for he can go just as far as his breath will take him.

This personal instrument of ours is again unique in that it embodies the principles of *every other* form of musical instrument, Wind, String and Percussion. Yet its mechanism, apparently so intricate, is so simple that the youngest child can manipulate it, for it is founded on the most rudimentary of sound-producers—the "penny whistle"!

And here is the final miracle. This instrument, so simple in design and so easy to play, can produce tones infinitely more subtle and varied than is possible for any made by man, and of a volume—if need be—capable of exceeding that of a full symphony orchestra.

Strange as it may seem, the apparent simplicity of speech is one of its chief problems.

To speak is the easiest process in the world, and the most difficult. Easy, in that every one around us is doing it too, and nothing is simpler than to "parrot" others; difficult, for that identical reason—because everyone is doing it, and it takes courage to be "different"—if what we are hearing around us is "poor stuff", as so much of it undoubtedly is.

There is no real excuse for this, for the overwhelming advantage that the Human Instrument enjoys over all the others is its *availability*. No special aptitude is required in order to master it, and no special time need be set aside for its practise—*we are practising all the time,* from morning till night, and, in fact, during the night (and I don't mean talking in our sleep) for breathing is an indispensable part of the process.

Our instrument has not to be selected and purchased; it

The Miracle of Speech

hasn't to be carried around in an awkward case; it demands no extra house-room; we are not compelled to make a journey to it, as the organist is to his organ. We are each born with one, perfect in construction, indestructible—if properly handled—and exclusively our own. In this universal possession all men are equal. *The only difference between one voice and another lies in the attitude of its owner*, the amount of thought given to its use. Whether we think of it merely as a series of vague, automatic noises that come-of-themselves whenever we want to make known our thoughts and wants, or as a vital and miraculous means whereby we can express the best in ourselves and bring out the best in others.

The mere possession of a voice is in itself a privilege when one considers the vocal limitations of animals and birds. These can only make their own characteristic sound, however diverse—and however urgent—the messages they strive to communicate. How thwarting, to have nothing from which to choose but a bark, a whine, or a growl. How bored the cuckoo must be with his two monotonous notes (reduced to one, in August); even the blackbird is restricted to the notes of all blackbirds; and as for the duck . . . These are indeed dumb.

I am never so grateful for the privilege of speech as when in the presence of the deaf and dumb, I feel awed, humbled by the responsibility of it—the obligation to use this marvellous faculty in the finest possible way. How dare we treat such a possession lightly, when there are those who are condemned never to use its powers for themselves nor to enjoy what is expressed through it by others? Hemmed in—gagged and bound—by silence. . . .

And yet there are countless *normal* people who go through life deaf to the sounds they are making, and without the slightest interest in how they make them—let alone how they affect other people.

As Cato said, nearly 2,000 years ago "Speech is the gift of all, but the thought of few."

1

Voice and Habit

SPEECH is the perfect means of expression. Even in the idioms of ordinary conversation we acknowledge this. We admire a portrait as a "Speaking likeness"; we say of a fine musician that his instrument "Speaks"....

Those of us who have the gift of expressing ourselves through other mediums—melody, colour, wood, fabric and so on—need to use speech as well. The spoken words provide the one clear route by which the ego within can escape into the world without—the living link between brain and brain, heart and heart, spirit and spirit. Your Voice *is* You.

Disraeli asserts that "There is no index of character so sure as the Voice," and certainly people assess us, more than anything else, according to our speech. Their first impressions may take note of our appearance and bearing, but those impressions can quickly fade—unless they are confirmed—immediately we open our mouths. My publisher tells me he has often decided how much credit to give to strangers on the phone by the sound of their voices and nothing else.

We all know something of the psychological effect of sound. How it can soothe or stimulate, vaguely depress or quite definitely jar the nerves. A moaning wind, a clanging bell, the sound of bees, aeroplanes, dipping oars, a distant train, or dog's bark—all have an influence on us, and an association.

Music plays a similar part in our thought. So does speech. A person's voice can attract or repell—largely because its tones carry a definite *association*.

Every voice unconsciously reflects its owner's prevailing mood. It tends to rise, for instance, when we are happy, to fall when we are sad. It follows that, if we have the *habit* of raising our voice, or of lowering it, we give the impression—

Voice and Habit

rightly or wrongly—of being the sort of person who is *habitually* gay (or excitable) or habitually gloomy (or bored).

Habits of Voice are inevitably associated with habits of mind, and what is character, but the sum-total of habitual thought?

Thus—and this is important—if your Voice is not being used naturally, if, through long habit, you play your instrument badly, you may be implying traits of character that are not really yours at all.

You may think your particular way of speaking is natural simply *because* it is habitual to you. You are used to it—everyone else is used to it—but are you satisfied with it? Probably not, or you would not be reading this book. *Your Natural Voice is perfect*, and if you are not absolutely happy about what it is doing for you at the moment, that indicates that something is wrong: something, probably, that has quite a simple explanation and that you will be foolish—for your own sake—not to put right.

For instance, supposing your voice is rather edgy and hard: it could quite easily give the impression that you are inclined to be nervy and bad tempered—whereas you are merely speaking through a contracted throat. If your tones are breathy and weak they might suggest to others that you are a feeble, unreliable type—simply because you are not making use of natural resonance. If your Speech is "woolly" and indistinct we might think you are also woolly-brained—when you are only failing to use your tongue and lips firmly.

Of course, you may possess one of these mental trends—which are consequently mirrored in the voice—on the other hand, you may not. How unfortunate, then—and how unnecessary—to give such a wrong and *detrimental* impression.

If our character is judged by our voice, it is entirely up to us whether or not that judgement is favourable. There is no need whatever for us to tolerate, in ourselves, speech habits that give the lie to our true nature, possibly affecting adversely all our human contacts.

There are obviously many psychological reasons for unnatural speech, but they need not be considered here. What

Release Your Voice and Find Your Personality

this book is concerned with is the Vocal results of these: and by tackling our inner problems via their outward manifestations we shall find we are treating the Causes themselves, for *our speech affects our thought just as much as our thought affects our speech.*

It has long been proved, in other spheres, that the inner self can definitely be "got at" through the training of the outer self. The concentrated effort necessary for any kind of physical control demands also a mental and moral striving that has an undoubted influence over the character. Hence the stress laid on sport in the education of youth. Self-discipline is essential, if we are to face up to the disciplines of life—(whatever educationalists may say in favour of free expression) . . . and Voice-discipline is an essential—though much neglected—part of it. It is so much easier to mumble than to speak out, to let one's words drop from slack lips instead of giving them form and shape, to slur them together instead of separating them cleanly—just as it is easier to slouch than to step smartly; to scribble, than to trace one's letters with care.

It is a matter, partly, of self-respect and of personal pride in what—as responsible individuals—we set ourselves to do. . . . But the influence of Better Speaking goes deeper than that. I have watched personalities wake up and blossom out, through *finding their true voice.* I have seen apparently dull people develop a new warmth of vitality, nervy people relax into serenity—and people tied-up with self-consciousness lose their fear of others—and of themselves—and find new freedom and happiness.

A Good Voice is our birthright. We are as naturally entitled to it as we are to a clear skin, smooth hands and healthy hair. We may not all be endowed with perfect features—certainly no baby is born with them; and he has next to no hair, and his voice is often far from musical—but it can be surprisingly strong and convincing! And his flesh is like silk, his complexion flawless. . . . All the *ingredients* for good health and good speech are there, awaiting development. How they develop depends on many things; on his environment, on his reaction to other

Voice and Habit

human beings, and on his own growing self awareness. But good health is natural, and poor health unnatural: it follows that a good voice is natural, and a poor one unnatural.

Admitted, some are born with a physique that makes good health easier, and similarly some are born with a physique that makes good speech easier. The shape of the mouth—inside as well as out—can affect both tone and clarity; the structure of head and shoulders, the size of the tongue, even the shape of the nose—all have their part to play in the making of the individual voice, as we shall presently discover.

But it is not so much what we have, as what we do with what we have, that matters—in speech, as in life.

This truth was brought home to me when I bought my first—and last—violin. Having very little knowledge of the instrument, I asked a musical friend to help me choose it. It was obviously a beauty and I was delighted. I bore it home in happy anticipation, tightened the strings, adjusted the bow, tucked my new treasure under my chin . . . The next five minutes revealed how little the quality of an instrument counts, lacking the skill of the player. I expected the whole thing to "come" without effort—as so many speakers do.

Because a good voice, like good speech, doesn't come-of-itself the average person is content to make do—or else he lacks the courage to do anything but make do—when it is within his power to develop almost any kind of voice he wishes for—at all events to improve his present speech 100 per cent. All he needs is an understanding of his instrument, plus a little imagination and patience: imagination—to hear mentally the kind of speech he desires; patience—to persevere with the simple disciplines necessary to achieve it.

Most people are interested in themselves. It is unaccountable that more people are not interested in their voice. The study is absolutely fascinating—and one that is also completely straightforward (at whatever age or stage we start) for we are dealing with something that is with us the whole of the time, part and parcel of our existence.

Possibly this is the main reason why so many people do "make do"—imagining that, because their Voice is already there—built in, so to speak—its particular characteristics are there for good (or for bad) and nothing much can be done about it. But much can be done, and much needs to be, judging by the strange noises to be heard around us in any public place. . . .

I never cease to wonder at the extraordinary variations of sound possible to the Human Instrument. One has only to sit in a café at rush hour, or on a crowded beach in summer, to realize that the voice is undoubtedly the most versatile of all musical—and unmusical—instruments. The diversities of the human face are staggering enough, when one considers the limitless changes rung on the simple Theme of eyes—nose—mouth: this very variety of feature being—as already hinted at—partly responsible for the amazing differences in human speech. (This is only one of the many surprises awaiting us in our studies. Another is that during the process of apparently changing our voice, we can, up to a point, even change our appearance!)

Unfortunately, no one ever hears his own voice exactly as it sounds to other people. It is a well-known fact that professional speakers and actors seldom recognize themselves the first time they hear their voices recorded. There are some perfectly common-sense reasons for this.

First of all, we are listening from *inside*, whereas everyone else is listening from outside; in other words, the sound vibrations, as we ourselves hear them, are bone-conducted, but once they leave us they are also affected by air-conduction, which considerably influences the tone. Again, we are *behind* the sounds, hearing them as they go from us, whilst they come *towards* those who are "out in front". Added to this, our own sounds are exceedingly *close*—literally on top of us—and nearness always tends to distort in sound as in vision. And anyway, we are so completely accustomed to the sound of our own speech—after all, it has been with us longer than we can remember—that we have become practically oblivious to it.

But even if we cannot hear ourselves as others hear us, we can still hear *a* voice, and by careful listening we can get a very good idea of its general characteristics. Is it loud or soft?

Voice and Habit

Is it vital, ponderous or whining? Are we drawlers or gabblers? Do we incline to the rumble or the squeak? (I spend much of my time hauling men's voices up and women's voices down.) When people are nervous they tend to use the extreme ends of their natural pitch: thus men tuck their chins into their collars and growl into their boots, and women tilt their chins and talk out of the top of their heads. And in normal, unanxious conversation there are many lazy voices that cling to the particular pitch that comes easiest, instead of making use of their whole vocal range.

Of course the chief reason we do not know ourselves, vocally, is that our mind is divided. How can we concentrate on what our voice is *doing* when our mind is already fully occupied with what that voice is *saying*?

We can only *hear* completely when we are able to listen completely, and naturally we are more concerned with the sense of our words than with their sound. Yet the two are one and inseparable. The sound conveys the sense; and if the sound is muffled, or slip-shod, or monotonous, then the sense is bound to suffer.

How can we remedy this? Only by doing one thing at a time.

We have two machines under our control, the Thought machine which looks after our ideas, and the Voice machine which is responsible for their communication. Both machines are directed by the Brain, but it can only *consciously* manage one machine at any one moment, so the work of the other must be done sub-consciously. It is obvious which one this has to be.

The Conscious Mind is the Creative Mind, and while we talk it is kept working at full pressure forming our thoughts, choosing our words, arranging our sentences. Therefore our Voice machine must be left to the mercy of the subconscious: to it is relegated the way we breathe, the way we resonate and the whole process of delivery. When we first learned to speak, this process was conscious and deliberate, but as we grew more fluent, and as our conscious interests in the life around us increased, so the elementary interests that once took up all our

Release Your Voice and Find Your Personality

time—learning to talk and walk and feed and dress oneself—were gradually taken over by the sub-conscious.

The Sub-conscious Mind is the Habit Mind. It cannot possibly create, but it can most faithfully reproduce; so the secret of good speech—and indeed, of good living—is to use our conscious mind to establish right habits, before handing them over to the sub-conscious for safe keeping.

Unfortunately in childhood the Talking Habit is often over-encouraged, and the Speaking Habit neglected. There is a world of difference between the two. We speak our *words*, we talk our *ideas*. Everyone knows how to talk, but how few of us—child or adult—know how to speak; this vital process is handed over, *far too soon*, to the Habit Mind—and we all know the tyranny of habits. They can become so much a part of us that we are no longer aware of their existence, and the deeper their roots, the harder they are to change. A Spanish proverb says—"Habits begin as cobwebs and end as cables."

Habits of speech are the most obstinate of all, simply because they start from our earliest years, to be repeated, and added to, every minute of every day. If an act twice repeated forms a habit, it is scarcely to be wondered at that acts of speech—a million times repeated—are difficult even to detect, let alone to alter. The phrase "force of habit" speaks for itself, but that force can be for good, if we will it so; and our present concern is to harness this force for the good of our Voice.

What good habits do we need to acquire? Habits for our breath, habits for our speech, habits for our words, even. Not the habit of using the *same* words—we shall make a habit of avoiding these—but the habit of choosing more apt and expressive ones, worthy of our new expressive voice. You will find that better *speaking* leads to better *talking*. As your voice improves you will be increasingly aware of the poor words you are asking it to utter, and so your conversation will improve, too: the conversation through which you reveal—and by which other people judge—your personality. . . .

We need to develop the habit of a rich, full voice—by *releasing* the natural tones that lie dormant in every Human

Voice and Habit

Instrument. These tones are awakened and nourished by the breath.

We need to acquire the habit of clear speaking—by the right and complete use of our speech muscles. This demands muscular energy—which is supplied by the breath.

We need a Voice that is vital and colourful—calling for the buoyancy of full breath support.

In addition to all this—if we are out to make the most of life—we need good health, good brains, and good nerves.

Breath is the source of every one of these, for it feeds not only the voice but the whole of our body, including the brain and the nervous system.

So the foundation of all our new Voice Habits will be knowledge and control of the breath.

2

The Breath of Life

BREATH is the power that makes Speech possible. Breath is the power that makes Life possible. It is essential to every living organism; even plants need to breathe. Without the breath of life, all life would cease on the earth.

Breath *is* Life. Without it man is no longer a being but a thing: "Thou takest away their breath, they die and return to their dust."

Those who have looked upon a lifeless face are often struck by its utter calm . . . But the lines of pain and anxiety have gone only because those lines were a part of the life that has gone: it is blankness that is left in their place. When there is no breath there is no individuality. Breath *is* Individuality.

Our individuality is three-fold, involving body, mind and spirit, and the breath feeds and nourishes them all. So before we study breathing as it affects our voice—the instrument mainly through which, our individuality is expressed—it is as well to know something about this wonderful power that passes through us, without ceasing, every moment of the day and night.

The average human being uses between 17 and 20 breaths a minute, and each of these consumes just over a pint of air. Thus we are gulping air at the rate of at least 20 pints a minute, or well over 1,000 pints an hour. I leave the reader to calculate the number of gallons imbibed per day, per week, per month, or year!

And what happens to these countless gulps of air? They seem merely to pass mechanically in and out of the top of the chest. Actually they are carried to every corner of our body via the blood, healing, renewing and vitalizing the tissues,

The Breath of Life

and most important—cleansing them, for there are millions of minute cells in the blood that collect up the waste products and carry them back to the lungs whence they are discharged on the exhaled breath.

We eat with our breath, for it is through the aerated red corpuscles of the blood that food is conveyed to sustain the body. Food does not fully nourish unless it is enjoyed. This enjoyment is largely dependent on the senses of taste and smell, and we *smell with our breath* through six little channelways called the posterior nares, situated at the rear of the nostrils. Up to a point, we can even *taste with our breath,* for many so-called tastes are actually odours, dependent on the sense of smell. (Without which there is said to be little difference between an apple and an onion!)

Now for the mental side. *We think with our breath,* for it is carried by the blood direct to the grey matter—the centre of activity in the brain. I knew of an author who always started his writing day by lying flat along the dining-room table with his head hanging over the edge—he maintained that the consequent rush of blood to the brain helped his thoughts to get going.... Certainly when the brain does not receive its full quota of aerated blood, our thinking suffers. If the air that feeds the brain is impure—due to a stuffy atmosphere—our concentration flags and we find ourselves nodding, and if the blood—aerated by our breath—begins to drain from the head, we actually lose consciousness in a faint.

Not only does the breath cleanse and nourish the body and vitalize the brain, it is inseparably bound up with our emotional life. It *reflects our reactions* to all that happens in our outer and inner world. Sometimes we express our feelings by drawing our breath *in,* sometimes by letting it *out,* sometimes by doing both; and by varying the speed of the breath—and the 'look' that goes with it—we can display a whole range of emotions without uttering a word.

We *inhale* once sharply—in other words, we gasp—in fear, or horror, or shock. (The instinct of self-preservation making us grab for extra life-power.) We inhale with a sipping sound, slowly, to convey sympathy; quickly, in protest against sudden

Release Your Voice and Find Your Personality

pain! We suck in our breath through pouted lips, with raised eyebrows, to indicate doubt.

We *exhale* quickly—through the nose—to show scorn; we puff out our cheeks and blow, with relief; we hiss in disapproval (except in Spanish theatres, where the audience hiss their applause!).

We breath in *and* out, deeply—that is, we sigh—not only to express sadness, but all sorts of other feelings, widely contrasted, according to our face and our pace! A *slow* sigh, with a smile, can mean contentment, or admiration; with a frown it can mean disappointment; with a shake of the head, disapproval; with a straight face and raised eyebrows, envy. Whereas a *quick* sigh signifies impatience!

We even *hold* our breath in apprehension, instinctively tightening our grip on our main source of strength.

We laugh with our breath. Have you ever paused to consider what a laugh really *is*? The mind is stimulated by something amusing—the heart beats faster—the blood circulates more swiftly—the breath comes quicker and finally overflows in a series of jerks. (A prosaic description of a stimulating emotional outlet!)

We *weep* by exactly the same physical process, the only difference being in the kind of stimulus that prompts it—a sad instead of a happy one—and in the facial expression that accompanies it. So close are these two physical "upheavals" that we sometimes laugh till we cry: the poet speaks of a joy that is akin to tears. . . .

Experiment for yourself. Let out a single "HA!" Breathe and let out two "HA's". Breathe again and let out three. Then alternate two and three quickly—with a smile—and you will be imitating what every actor does when he simulates laughter on the stage. Repeat the process with a frown and you will be weeping. Change to a smile again, but keep the mouth closed, and you will produce a giggle!

Sobbing, usually the aftermath of weeping, might be called weeping in reverse. So much breath has been expended that it is forced to renew itself, with rasping intakes—uneven and painful—because the mechanism is momentarily out of control.

The Breath of Life

Experiment again. Exhale first, then take in the breath in a series of short gasps ... You have learnt the art of laughing and crying at will!

But joy and grief are two of the most obvious emotions—there are many others, all expressed by the breath. Can you think of any? It is important to know about them. Why? Because the fact that we express emotion via the breath means that in learning how to control our breath, we are also learning how to control our emotions. Not to *repress* them, but to be master of them, and therefore to be master of something that plays a very large part in the forming of personality.

The advice "when angry take a deep breath and count ten" is wiser than many people realize, for it is based on a fundamental truth. ...

Most significant of all, and of paramount importance to the process of Speech—as we shall presently learn—is the fact that we *yawn* with our breath.

I have collected over two dozen different reasons for yawning —there are probably more—the three most obvious being tiredness, boredom and fug! Others include nervousness, hunger, indigestion, loss of blood and change of altitude (I learnt the last two from a nurse and an airman). Doubtless the reader can add to these. But whatever the immediate source of the yawn, it always has the same basic cause— insufficient breath. Our breathing has become so shallow that Nature steps in and demands more air—and proceeds to help herself by throwing open our mouth *and throat* and forcibly-feeding our lungs—right down to the level of the diaphragm.

And now comes another significant fact. The diaphragm, the chief of the breathing muscles, is closely connected with the Solar Plexus, the centre of the nervous system. Thus, in learning to control our breath, we shall also be learning to control our nerves—that modern whipping boy, blamed for so many of our everyday ills! "Take three deep breaths when nervous" is another wise old saying and we shall soon be proving its truth.

And what of the Spiritual Significance of our breath? Space does not permit more than a brief mention of this, but that it has such a significance is proved by the Yogis, whose age-old system has many adherents and is growing in popularity in Western Countries.

Can it be by chance that the Latin word for breath is *spiritus*, and the verb *aspirare* means to breathe? From this is derived the English verb to *aspire*—to reach for the highest. . . .

Again, the French word for breathing is *esprit*, and has not our own word *inspiration* a dual meaning—the receiving of breath into the body, and the receiving of higher influences into the mind? It is not the purpose of this book to sermonize, so I leave these thoughts with you. In another volume it may be possible to go into them more deeply. We pass on now to the purely physical aspect of breathing, exactly how it takes place, and how the Voice rides upon it.

Breath enters the body via mouth or nose, and travels down the windpipe to the lungs. On its return journey it can either exit silently through mouth or nose, or, on its way, it can come into contact with the vocal cords and emerge as sound.

This is a very elementary description of a very wonderful process, which we shall presently study in detail. *Suffice to say, at the moment, that the* amount *of breath we let in and out, and the* manner *in which we allow it to enter and exit, exactly determine the amount of voice that results and the quality of its sound, for Breath is Voice.*

The lungs are never empty, and never still. Whether we are awake or asleep, vigorously active or completely unconscious, they continue their vital task of renewing the air we breathe. This air is stored in our lungs in three layers, and their names indicate their nature. At the top is the Tidal air, which comes and goes rhythmically like the tides of the sea, and which is used for the light breathing of sleep and inactivity. Below this is the Reserve air—the main reservoir which, when renewed by a deep breath, is replaced by what is called the Complimental air. At the base of the lungs, almost level with the waist, is the Residual air, seldom renewed save in moments of extreme physical stress: it is the air that brings the drowning man to the surface for the third time; the final gasp that

The Breath of Life

produces what is known, somewhat gruesomely, as the death rattle.

The Tidal and Residual air together represent only one-fifth of our lung capacity, four-fifths are taken up by the Reserve air, the part that should continuously be renewed if we are to use our breath to full advantage. Yet it is a medical fact that the average person uses only the Tidal air for the greater part of his existence. The more active we are, the more breath we need, and this is when the trouble arises. We try to make a small amount of breath do a large amount of work, (like piling our car with luggage and then expecting the engine to run on a dribble of petrol), and when, at moments of *extra* physical stress, we find the supply of breath running short, we still cling to the wrong end of our breathing apparatus, quickening the breath instead of deepening it, raising the shoulders and dragging it in, using the unnatural suction created by a narrowed throat, instead of the natural, easy suction of fully expanding lungs.

Now, the lungs occupy the torso right from neck to waist, but the Tidal air expands them little below the level of the collar-bone, so that—worst error of all—the use of this clavicular breath, as it is called, means that the greater part of the air in our lungs is never renewed.

We are regularly refeeding our body and brain—and our voice—with stale air, that is, with carbon-di-oxide, which is virtually poison.

Strange, that the easiest job in the world should be done so badly! The first thing we do when we enter this life; the last thing we do before we leave it, and we trouble so little as to *how* we do it. Perhaps because it is so easy. The air is always there, whenever we want it, and we take it for granted, oblivious of its value; content with niggardly sips instead of the deep stimulating draughts that envigorate the body, steady the nerves, and vitalize the speech.

It might be argued that breathing is a subconscious function, why should we need to *learn* to do it correctly? Why do we make such elementary mistakes if Nature intended otherwise? Surely, if she is in charge of the process, she can be trusted to

Release Your Voice and Find Your Personality

get on with her job? Of course she can be trusted. The trouble is that we *don't* trust her, chiefly because we do not know enough about her. We know only the breath we can *see*—the shallow rise and fall at the top of the chest, whereas the true breath, the breath of better health and better speaking, is neither seen nor heard, coming deep and effortless from the centre of our being, like Tennyson's tide, "Too full for sound..."

There are occasions when we all get the urge to breathe deeply; on stepping out of a stuffy building into the cool evening air, or on that single rare morning which comes, just once, in the early part of the year, when "all suddenly the wind blows soft, and Spring is here again". We sigh "Ah... marvellous" and drink in the marvel, quickened in body and uplifted in spirit. Then a March wind comes round the corner; up go our collars, down go our heads, and we breathe into scarves—behind handkerchiefs—anything rather than face the clean wholesome air straight from the sky! The very Breath of God. . . . It is not enough to breathe deeply on sweet Spring mornings and still summer evenings, there are too few of them in our British climate. We should cultivate the habit of fully expanding our lungs *all the time*, walking or sitting, indoors or out, for the cold air will not harm us if we breathe it in the right way.

At the outset we must get rid of the idea—firmly implanted in our youthful minds at P.T.—that breath is something that has to be *taken*, and taken with effort, usually, in a long-drawn sniff, on tip-toe, with arms extended sideways... The fallacy that one should "Take a Deep Breath" is at the root of much wrong breathing, and of many nervous complaints besides. The phrase ought never to have got into our language. Deep breathing is natural breathing, and requires no physical effort on our part, only an effort of will.

Our lungs want to breathe deeply, as we soon discover when we try to hold our breath for any length of time. And this will be our first experiment—to hold the breath till we can no longer retain it, and then observe what takes place after its release. Try it as you read these words. . . . The breath, when it at last

The Breath of Life

escapes, rushes from the body, and is immediately replaced by a fresh lungful (the Complimental air) without any effort whatever. But *where were you conscious of movement!* NOT at the base of the neck, where the poor little Tidal air is so often grabbed at, and not at the abdomen (intended by Nature for quite another purpose), but deep in the chest—the main reservoir—where your Reserve air is stored.

Now experiment with your Residual air, that third layer stagnant at the base of the lungs. Forcefully expel the whole of your breath, through well-opened lips, completely emptying the lungs . . . When every scrap has gone, relax and observe. You will feel your sides swell outwards, evenly and firmly; you will experience a sensation not merely of relief but of well-being, and you will realize again how needless it is to "take a breath". Nature abhors a vacuum, and there is absolutely no point in taking by force what she is waiting to give.

If you find your chest rising instead of your sides expanding, you have not exhaled *completely*. To remedy this, place the fists against the lower ribs, just below the breasts, and press hard as you breathe out. When no more breath will come, release the pressure but retain the fist position so that you can feel the ribs swing out again. Repeat this pressure-and-release several times rhythmically . . . do you realize that you are imitating the movements of artificial respiration. Movements that obviously aim to reproduce *natural* breathing as closely as possible. Note that the rescuer does not work upon the neck and shoulders or even the chest of his casualty—he lays the body face downwards. Note, too, that *the emptying comes first*, so that the following fill up (or rather fill-out) is achieved by the ribs natural rebound. This is the first principle of Better Breathing—that the breath should pass out and in, *not* in and out. The stale air must be expelled before the clean air can enter, so the act of breathing is just this—continuously and rhythmically creating a vacuum that Nature at once rushes to fill.

INCIDENTALLY, TO BREATH OUT-AND-IN IS A TREMENDOUS HELP WHEN HURRYING, OR WALKING UPHILL. IT COMPLETELY ELIMINATES THAT RASPING

Release Your Voice and Find Your Personality

IN-TAKE WHICH HURTS THE THROAT AND STRAINS THE HEART. CONCENTRATE ON THE EXHALING—DO IT WITH ALL YOUR FORCE—THEN MERELY *RECEIVE* THE FRESH BREATH. . . . CONTINUE RHYTHMICALLY—SAY, THREE STEPS OUT, THREE STEPS IN—AND YOU WILL FIND YOURSELF MUCH LESS OUT-OF-BREATH.

For the sake of your health as well as your voice, try the following simple recipe twice a day—first thing in the morning, and again last thing at night, stand at the open window and completely empty your lungs once. During sleep, inevitably, the stale breath accumulates below the level of the sub-conscious Tidal air. Get rid of it at the earliest opportunity so as to start the day with your lungs *filled* with the Breath of Life. During the day the poison will pile up again (until you have formed the *habit* of breathing deeply): dispel it all before you get into bed. The clean cool Complimental air that takes its place will help you to sleep soundly, possibly even to live longer! A French doctor, aged 92, has declared that any normal person could live to be 100, and those who don't, just kill themselves by breath-starvation. I would add—by breath-poisoning, for the shallow air we *do* inhale—in public vehicles and public buildings, places of work and places of entertainment—is too often contaminated from use and re-use.

Clean air is especially important at night. A stuffy bedroom, where we spend one-third of our life, affects the quality of our sleep: respired air is a drug from which we awake muggy and unrefreshed.

The first few moments in bed are a most useful odd-time for trying out the few simple breathing experiments outlined in this and the following chapter. All the muscles are relaxed, so you can concentrate wholly on the particular ones concerned. Lie flat on your back, for then the body is in the ideal breathing position—spine straight, shoulders level, no strained neck or bulging tummy . . .

Look after your breathing and your breathing will look after you.

3

Our Wind Instrument

A GLANCE at the "works" will show how the whole structure of our breathing mechanism is designed expressly for the deeper, fuller breath. Our two lungs are roughly pear-shaped, narrow at the top, wide at the base, and contain innumerable cells, like sponges, that expand and fill with air instead of water. The air enters them via the windpipe—a river of breath whose main stream forks when it reaches the chest, one stream entering each lung, there it divides and divides again into smaller tributaries that penetrate every corner.

The lungs are exceedingly delicate, but nature shields them well, as she does all the vulnerable parts of our body, and the more vital their function, the stronger their covering. The brain is protected by the hard sheath of the skull; the eyes by eyelids, lashes and brow; and the lungs and heart by a great cage of bone, the ribs. This cage is made up of twenty-four bars

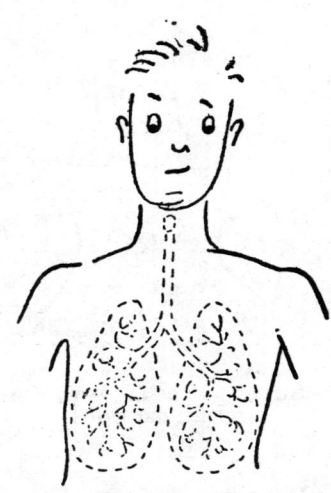
Our lungs are pear-shaped.

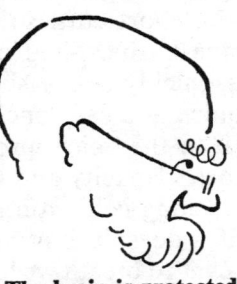
The brain is protected by . . . the skull.

The eyes by . . . lashes.

of bone encircling the body, twelve each side, attached to the backbone behind and, except for the lowest ones, to the breastbone in front. They are linked between by elastic muscles that contract and expand as the air leaves and enters.

The ribs are graded in size to follow the shape of the lungs, so the upper ones are short and close together, and the muscles between them have little play; the lower ones are longer and farther apart, and the muscles are capable of wider and stronger movement, but because they are fixed back and front their expansion is still limited. The breastbone being shorter than the backbone, however, there are several pairs of ribs "left over" on each side, which are *free* in front and thus able to expand much more easily; in fact, the lowest "floating ribs" will stretch just as far as we can stretch our skin... So you see, our body simply isn't built for shallow breathing, for these three obvious reasons—that at the top of the chest the lungs are at their narrowest, the ribs at their smallest and the muscle actions at their most limited.

Stretch ... as far as we can stretch our skin!

It seems curious that Clavicular breathing should be so prevalent when everything is against it! But man is a lazy animal and loves to take short cuts, so he uses just that bit of lung space nearest the business-end of speech in order to "get at" his breath as quickly and easily as possible. Yet a deep breath is just as quick and easy once the habit is formed, and much more helpful to the voice, provided we keep three things in mind—Comfort, Capacity and Control.

Comfort, because breathing is a natural process and should therefore *feel* natural, if it doesn't, it is wrong.

Capacity, because the more breath we have, the more life and energy we have, and the more voice.

Our Wind Instrument

Control, because what we do with the breath is even more important than its amount.

COMFORTABLE BREATHING

Comfort comes from doing it in the right place in the right way, and for true comfort there should be, first of all, no tenseness of any kind. Relaxation is not so simple as it sounds. Magazines are always preaching it, numerous methods are advocated, yet one still hears the regular complaint "If only I could relax..." Even in bed we find ourselves with shoulders hunched, fists clenched, knees drawn up, toes curled.

THE ABILITY TO "LET GO" IS AS RARE AS IT IS VALUABLE, BUT IT *CAN* BE CULTIVATED.

The art of relaxing, physical and mental, is a study in itself, and this must wait for another book. Of direct importance to us now is the fact that *most states of tension concentrate themselves around the centre of speech*. In other words, the throat muscles around the voice box (or Adam's apple), the jaw above it, and the shoulders below it are the first things to tighten, and the last things to loosen. No wonder some people lose their voice after periods of stress....

So, for a start, consciously drop your shoulders right now, and ungrit your teeth! It is not necessary to clench the jaw whenever the mouth is closed. Yet many of us do. I knew a teacher who complained that he always had jaw-ache on Sunday nights. It seemed that this was the time when he caught up with his private correspondence; it was usually pretty heavy, his time was limited, and he loathed writing letters! (Incidentally, his speech was hard and throaty, and he lost his voice regularly at the end of every term. Some of the prescriptions contained in these pages, helped to put him right.)

Make a habit of dropping the shoulders and unclenching the teeth whenever you think of it, especially while sitting at ease when there is no reason for any tenseness, and make another habit of always sitting well back in your seat, so that the spine is supported from the base up—*a relaxed body is not a collapsed body.*

Release Your Voice and Find Your Personality

Many of us have sedentary occupations, and all of us spend a great deal of our time in a sitting position—in vehicles, restaurants, and places of entertainment—consequently we have acquired the habit of sagging in the middle, sitting (and walking) with our waists sunk into our hips, like eggs in eggcups. To breath deeply and fully in this position is a positive effort, for our ribs have the extra task of lifting the chest and pushing the tummy out of the way before the lungs can start their sideways swing. No wonder we resort to breathing either above or below the sag! And so our middle thickens and stiffens, and we develop a "rubber tyre" just where the body needs to be most pliable.

Pull yourself out of your hips, so that the floating ribs have room to move. There should be an area at least four inches deep between waist and chest—we call it the Breath Belt. To widen this "belt", try stretching the body between waist and armpits by lifting first one shoulder then the other as high as it will go, and then relaxing it *back*. Now, slowly rotate both shoulders as though unwinding yourself. When you can't "unwind" any further, rest the two shoulders back so that your body is supported by your spine, as Nature intended it to be. There is no need to sit stiffly—use your backbone to *rest* on, and you will soon find it more comfortable than any artificial support.

Wear this "Breath Belt" when you are out walking. It will give your body a new balance and ease of movement—and also help to narrow your waist-line.

At first you may feel a slight strain in the small of the back—the muscles between the vertibrae are so unused to being stretched—but the general feeling will be one of buoyancy and support.

Everyone admires a graceful carriage. So much of a person's character is implied by his walk, especially from behind, where there is no face to detract! If you find yourself judging someone by his walking back-view, remember others may be judging you by yours! Do you transfer your weight alternately from one foot to the other, as though your body was designed from a child's drawing with a leg on each corner? Beware! you

Our Wind Instrument

are heading (or rather, legging) for a waddle. . . . The body should be poised centrally over the hip-bone, floating above the legs, so to speak, as they move rhythmically below. Buoyed up by the Breath Belt, as it were by a life-belt, you will feel you are literally walking-on-air!

But don't sag directly you get indoors again. Stop yourself slumping about the home or the office, and at the meal table especially. It is quite remarkable how badly the average

How badly the average person sits to eat.

person sits to eat, stooping over the plate with the body curved just where it should be straightest, at the vital area which is the centre not only of the breath, and of the nerves and emotions, but also of the digestion. This explains why some of us can't eat when emotionally upset—hence the term "nervous indigestion".

Good posture is an asset at all times. It gives moral as well as muscular support, helping us to sit and stand firm in both senses of the term! Especially if we combine it with deep out-and-in breathing. Test this in the Dentist's waiting room, or the next time you have an important interview—any occasion when you are inclined to nervousness or apprehension. A poised body promotes a poised mind, and an even breath keeps the pulse even. . . .

The whole of our breathing apparatus being situated above the waist, there is no reason why we should not sit for the

Release Your Voice and Find Your Personality

experiments that follow—provided we sit well—and we can just as easily rehearse them at odd moments during the day—in public, if need be—as at set times in private (which probably means not at all). Why relegate to a special time something that should be happening all the time? We *have* to breathe—wherever we are, whatever we are doing—so why not get into the way of doing it properly, at every available opportunity?

Having *made room* for the breath, the next step is to *enlarge* it. This means developing the flexibility of our lower ribs so that the lungs behind them can stretch more fully.

To locate them inconspicuously (if you are rehearsing at a bus-stop, for instance!) tuck the thumbs in the lower waistcoat pockets, or lift the forearms parallel with the waist and rest the wrists against the body with hands lightly clasped.

Breathe *out* firmly, *in* gently (as for the Artificial Respiration experiment) mentally counting a slow three, each way. Do this three times; then increase to four each way, then five, and so on.

The emptying breath must always be the *active* movement, and the filling breath the passive one. Why? Because it is this emptying breath that carries the Voice, and if the breath is feeble so will be the sounds that ride upon it. Don't strain for a high number of counts—be content with—say—seven, at the moment—or you may find you are merely holding-on to yourself when the lungs are already empty, or full. Keep the breath moving, and keep it in the Breath Belt—that is, don't allow the chest to rise, and guard against any expansion *below* the waist. The tummy muscles are notoriously weak, or they would not need artificial support; they expand easily, but they also collapse easily and the breath collapses with them.

Abdominal breathing, besides being bad for the figure—developing that portion of the anatomy which most of us are anxious to reduce—gives no control over the outgoing breath and therefore no control over the voice.

You may find the ribs rather reluctant at first (like new rubber hot-water-bottles, unused to being filled) but they will soon respond, with a little regular use. Try stretching and releasing them, at odd moments, independent of the breath, thinking only of the muscular action.

Our Wind Instrument

As a follow-on to the Rhythmic Breath routine, breathe out for three counts—in for *four*; out for five—in for six, etc. Concentrate hard on the outflow and you will probably reach ten this time, for *the more you breathe out, the more you breathe in.*

One further aid to Capacity Breathing. Empty evenly and fully for three counts—remain empty for three; refill for three—stay full for three. Do the same for four counts, then five, not more. The point here, is that the empty lungs *want* to fill and the full lungs want to empty, so after each pause the ribs will swing all the more swiftly into the opposite position.

Avoid any tension during the pauses—and don't feel you are *holding* the breath—just let the mind dwell calmly on what is happening. The *emptied* lungs, clear of impurities, are quietly awaiting a new, clean breath charged with vitality; and the *filled* lungs are quietly enjoying that breath, letting it permeate every cranny. . . .

BREATH FOR SPEAKING INVOLVES A TWO-WAY TRAFFIC —THE INFLOW TO CARRY THE "FUEL", THE OUTFLOW TO CARRY THE VOICE.

So, having found out where our fuel can be stored comfortably, and how to enlarge our storage space, we now turn our attention to controlling our use of it.

It is here that a word might be said as to the relative virtues of nose and mouth breathing. The nostril breath is undoubtedly the more hygienic of the two. The back of the nose is fitted with fine filters—which prepare the harsh air for the delicate lungs, instantly and miraculously warming, softening and cleansing it. Compare the effect of the two passage-ways for yourself. Inhale swiftly through the mouth and you can feel the cold air against tongue and roof. Inhale again, lips closed, and the entering air is hardly detectable. But whenever we breathe in order to speak, the breath instinctively enters the mouth, for three perfectly common sense reasons: the hole is bigger, the journey to the lungs is shorter, and the lips are already apart in anticipation of our next word. Also, nose-breathing tends to lower the soft palate—that is, the back of the roof of the mouth—partly shutting off the mouth exit.

Release Your Voice and Find Your Personality

This means the voice must find another way out, resulting in a nasal quality that is not particularly pleasant.

Whilst our thoughts are concerned with breathing for health's sake, it is as well to use the healthier method (provided we avoid tensing the lips and nostrils and *sniffing* the air in). But as soon as we consider it in direct relation to speech, we should switch to mouth-breathing. It seems only sensible to practise what is bound to take place in the end—unless, of course, we happen to be rehearsing at some odd moment outdoors on a cold day!

How Breath is actually converted into Sound we shall discover in the next chapter, but it is obvious that the one effects the other. Whether the outgoing air is steady, or violent, or uneven, or weak, the tone it carries is bound to be likewise, and so we must now learn to *regulate* our increased supply of air on its return journey up the windpipe.

Left to themselves, the ribs tend to collapse by their own weight, and the lungs with them (the reason our voice sometimes fades out before the end of a sentence). Their movement has to be regulated by means of the intecostals—as the muscles between the ribs are called—working in conjunction with the diaphragm. This wonderful muscle extends right across the centre of our body, in that important area which houses such vital organs as the heart and the stomach. You can feel it just below the breastbone in the triangular space between the floating ribs—like the buckle of your breath belt. Think of the lower ribs encircling your body like a deep elastic belt held by an expanding metal clasp, and you have some idea of the strength and significance of the diaphragm in relation to breathing—and to the whole of the nervous system.

Rest the finger-tips against it during the next two experiments—this helps to direct your mind towards its control.

Exhale completely, allow the lungs to re-expand, then open the lips and release the breath slowly but with a gentle force —as if you were breathing on your hands to warm them, or making steam on a window-pane—producing a whispered "HAH . . ." Don't hold back the breath, or there will be no strength in it, and *feeble breath means feeble tone*. The air

Our Wind Instrument

must escape, the aim is for it to escape *steadily*—during a mental count of about ten.

Press the diaphragm gently as you exhale, at the same time keeping the ribs expanded, so that their weight does not hurry the breath out. Think of it this way—that as the breath enters, your waist-belt expands, and as the breath exits again, your body remains *wide* but becomes gradually *thinner* from front to back, till you feel like a cardboard figure—with the stomach practically meeting the backbone!

If you find difficulty in "keeping wide" you can help to strengthen the rib muscles by consciously holding them stretched for short periods, any time it occurs to you. (There is no need to hold the breath while doing this.)

Exhale and expand as before, and this time let out the breath on a steady HISS. Avoid tightening the lips or jaw, or the throat may tighten in sympathy, and *a restricted throat means restricted tone*. Try to keep the Hiss uniform in strength —for about fifteen mental counts. (The breath should last longer, now that the mouth-exit is smaller.) Change the "SS" to "TH", in public, and it will be undetectable!

A good way to keep the silent counting regular is mentally to add the word "thousand" after each number—"one-thousand, two-thousand", etc. I am told bomb throwers used to be trained to do this. The missile is timed to explode at so many seconds after the pin is removed, and a fraction's miscalculation might mean disaster—if thrown too soon it can be caught and thrown back; if thrown too late . . .

The easiest way to regulate your counting is to fit in with the footsteps. Walking is a grand opportunity for improving the breath control. We speak of a walk as a "breather"— it can be literally that. Climbers breathe in rhythm with their steps. The great Mountaineers go further and synchronize both breath and stride with the heart-beat.

Breathing-while-you-walk shortens a long tramp and enlivens a dull one, and you finish up surprisingly fresh, especially if you make it a *mental* "breather" as well as a physical one: after an upset, emotional or digestive, do you like to "walk-it-off"? Does going-for-a-walk help you to settle a problem?

Release Your Voice and Find Your Personality

Let your breathing help, too—don't forget to lift out of the waist and rest back on the spine as you start out, and remember always, to breathe *out and in*. Set up a comfortable rhythm, say, four-firm-steps-out . . . four-firm-steps-in . . .

REMIND YOURSELF, WITH EACH EMPTYING BREATH, THAT YOU ARE ALSO EMPTYING AWAY ALL THE ACHES AND GERMS AND NERVES, ALL THE DEPRESSION AND LASSITUDE; AND WITH EACH INFLOW THAT YOU ARE RECEIVING NEW VITALITY FROM THE BREATH OF LIFE THAT SURROUNDS US—THE UNIVERSAL ENERGY THAT DRAWS THE FLOWERS FROM THE EARTH AND HOLDS THE LARK IN THE SKY AND BLOWS THE FOUR WINDS ACROSS THE WORLD. LET THIS REALIZATION FLOOD YOUR BEING AS AIR FLOODS YOUR VEINS.

TELL YOURSELF YOU ARE BREATHING NOT JUST TO RETAIN LIFE BUT TO *LIVE* IT, AND LIVE IT MORE ABUNDANTLY. THAT YOU ARE BREATHING TO BENEFIT YOUR BODY AND BRAIN AS WELL AS YOUR SPEECH, AND THAT EVERY LUNGFUL OF AIR IS HELPING TO ENRICH NOT ONLY YOUR VOICE BUT YOUR WHOLE PERSONALITY.

4

The Door of the Voice

THE only good speech is natural speech, resulting from a voice produced and used as Nature intended it to be. We know, now, how to breathe naturally, using the natural movement of the lungs and ribs according to their natural build, and so far we have concentrated on the *lower* end of our speech apparatus, learning how to increase our stock of air and how to regulate its flow.

But however big the container, it cannot be filled or emptied *easily* unless it has an adequate opening, so we now turn to the *top* end of the apparatus—not the mouth (as yet), but the throat.

The most frequent fault in the using of the voice is throat-contraction. It is at the root of nearly all speech troubles (as distinct from speech errors) of which the most general are inadequate breath, hard tone, thin quality, sore throat and loss of voice. Inadequate breath—because the air has to squeeze its way through; hard tone—because the voice has to do the same; thin quality—because there is no room for the voice to expand; sore throat—because its muscles are strained by continual tightening; and loss of voice—because wrongly treated it just cannot stand up to the stress of continual use.

Such are the results—but what is the *reason* for throat contraction? Fundamentally, I would say, because the pace of modern life is such, that most of us live in a constant state of tension; always hurrying—because everyone else is hurrying—our minds tense, and our bodies tense even in apparent repose; and the voice being the chief means by which we tense individuals express ourselves, it is no wonder that the throat—the voice's channel way, and one of the most sensitive areas of the body—reacts in sympathy.

Release Your Voice and Find Your Personality

Speaking through a closed throat is like trying to converse through a closed door. How can we open the door comfortably, so that a full breath may enter—and *keep* the door open, without strain, so that a full tone may exit?

As always, in this book, we look for the natural way. Nature opens our throat and fills our lungs easily and *instantly* every time she causes us to yawn. So simple is the process that it is usually half over before we even realize it is happening....

When people complain to me of tired voice, or breathlessness, or throat-ache, or any of the 101 vocal maladies caused by throat-constriction my first request is to look into their mouth. Usually, all I see is a hill of pink flesh, the tongue curving up to meet the roof curving down—the door tight shut against the breath that wants to go in and the voice that wants to come out, like the first of the interior views below.

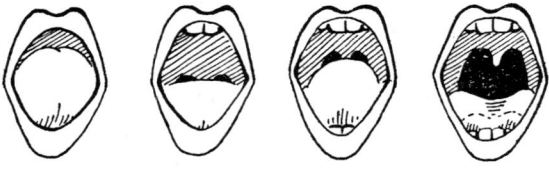

Which of these four "views" do you see?

Look inside your own mouth, with the aid of a mirror.

Which of these four views do you see?

(If it is the last one, you may like to skip the next few pages, and resume at page 46.)

Possibly you will see the second interior, with tongue level and roof only partially sagged, revealing a glimpse of uvula. Now take a quick breath (an instruction that will never again appear in the volume!) and you will probably see interior three, the roof well raised, but the tongue raised with it, drawn back by the inward drag of the breath.

But now imitate a yawn—a slow deep one—and watch for the transformation; the roof should arch, the uvula shoot upwards (or even disappear) and the tongue become concave

The Door of the Voice

—opening the door wide. What could be easier? Better still, what could be more natural?

But the yawn is an involuntary reaction to certain conditions: it is "on us" unawares. Our task is to make it a *voluntary action* under all conditions—until habit relegates it to the subconscious—so that, with our throat always poised for a yawn, so to speak, breath and voice can pass through unimpeded. This does not mean that we have to go about opening and closing our mouths like gold-fish! It is quite possible to yawn with the lips very slightly parted; it is even possible to yawn with mouth closed—through distended nostrils—as we are sometimes forced to do in polite but boring company. (Though this flattens the soft palate, as already mentioned.) And it is perfectly possible, with a little perseverance, to adopt the yawn-position of tongue and palate behind closed lips, without any inflow of breath: all of which can be rehearsed at odd moments, anywhere.

To begin with, do this little routine once a day, when you happen to be in front of a shaving mirror, or using a powder compact:
1. Yawn in, with mouth and throat wide open.
2. Close the eyes and register the *sensation* of concave tongue and arched palate.
3. Relax, then—still with eyes closed—try to reproduce the sensation with muscle action *only*.
4. Open eyes and check up. . . .

Try repeating the muscle action three times quickly, first with mouth half-closed, then with lips together but teeth apart (to avoid a rigid jaw). Also try *holding* the yawn position for short periods (without necessarily holding the breath) and if a genuine yawn interrupts, you will know you have it right— your muscle work was so realistic that Nature couldn't resist.

But perhaps these mock-yawns do not come very easily? If the tongue darts in every direction save the one you want, and the uvula just bounces up and down (chiefly down), then a little knowledge of mouth mechanics may help.

The roof has two sections, as you can feel if you pass your

Release Your Voice and Find Your Personality

tongue over it. The front, just behind the teeth, is known as the hard palate, a rigid dome that provides a natural sounding board for the voice (which we shall learn to use in the "loud-speaker" chapter).

Further back is the soft palate, where the roof is muscular and pliable but tends, in repose, to sag towards the back of the tongue so that its tail-end, the uvula is lowered into the throat opening, forming an effective "stopper" for both breath and voice (as in the bottom sketch on page 45).

To prevent this we must first tackle the tongue, for until that is out of the way, we cannot see what the uvula is up to.

The tongue has more muscles, in relation to its size, than any other single part of the body, and when we try consciously to control it, the tendency is for all its muscles to start working at once! Dentists have continually to cope with this—dodging people's tongues with their little mirror. My dentist and I agree how handy it would be if tongues were detachable, and doctors often have to depress the blade with a spatula in order to see down a patient's throat. If your tongue refuses to lie down, anchor it with your little finger, letting the muscles relax around it. Some people can flute the tongue without a thought, others find it a considerable effort. It may help if you protrude it first, and then draw it slowly back into the mouth, curving the sides up as it retreats. Often people who can't "flute", can't whistle, and whistling—even if you fail to produce a tune—is an excellent way of developing tongue control.

Some flute their tongue without a thought.

Others find it a considerable effort.

But here is another difficulty. The tongue actually is a little too long for the mouth! This is not a mistake on Nature's part, it is necessary for the various demands of speech and mastication, but when inactive, these extra inches—or fractions of an inch—must be housed somewhere. We can't hang

The Door of the Voice

out our tongue like a dog does, instead, most of us either hump it towards the back, blocking the throat opening, or else shorten it by letting it thicken, so that it fills the mouth, blocking the tone.

The secret is in the correct placing of the front edge, which should rest forward—tipped very slightly upward—against the lower front teeth, allowing the centre of the tongue to sink, concave, into the natural saucer of the lower jaw,

like this—   **not this—**

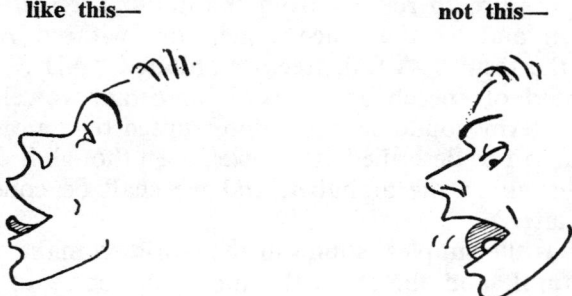

Having opened the throat half-way by lowering the floor, we can now see to raise the roof! This requires control of certain muscles of the soft palate, called the Pillars of the Fauces. They are on either side, parallel with the tonsils, and they do the work literally, of pillars, in that when stretched, they support the arched opening of the throat.

To make both roof and floor more flexible, repeat "NG-AH"! vigorously. NG brings palate and tongue together, AH shoots them apart, thus:

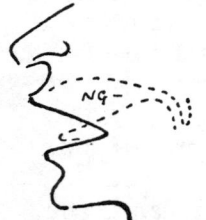 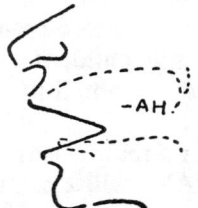

NG brings palate and tongue together.   **AH shoots them apart.**

Release Your Voice and Find Your Personality

This can be rehearsed at odd moments, quite inconspicuously—in a whisper with lips closed: but at first you may need to watch the movements in a mirror, and if the tongue seems to be doing most of the work—press your little finger firmly along it so that the pillar muscles are made to do their share.

Once this "back door" of the mouth is under control we are ready, at last, to release our natural voice.

Indulge in a single, deep, really bad-mannered yawn—that is, when the breath returns from the lungs, keep the mouth wide open and let the voice come, too, without restraint. What is the result? A full, free, uninhibited "AH . . .!" the basic sound of speech and a very important vowel in our language. (Any sound that is uninterrupted by action of lips or tongue can be described as a vowel, even though it does not actually occur in the alphabet, and we shall be considering them all later.)

"AH" is the simplest sound in the world to make, and the most natural, and therefore the most conducive to natural tones. It is the first sound we utter when we enter this life—and the last when we leave it: the newly born baby is slapped into crying it—with no uncertain voice—the newly dead body emits it when first moved. (A fact learned from the medical profession—not from personal experience.) Doctors ask us to say it when they want to examine our throat. Singers use it for nearly all their exercises. A musical friend has suggested that the lack of word clarity all too common among vocalists is due to what he calls the "AH complex". They practise so much on this particular sound that it colours—or rather un-colours—their whole performance, nearly every vowel being distorted more-or-less to conform to it. I vividly remember as a child, hearing the refrain of a then-popular ballad rendered something like this:

> "To mah-i heart ah-i will prah-ss you,
> Ah-i will kiss arnd ca-rah-ss you.
> So goodnah-it arnd Gard blah-ss you,
> Ah-i will see you tonah-it"!

. . .

The Door of the Voice

But to return to our "rude" yawn. Repeat it several times—with mouth and throat well open, and accompanied by good, wide rib swings—making each "AH" longer and stronger. Don't let the pitch rise—deepen it, rather (no one likes a high penetrating voice, everyone admires a low mellow one) but don't swallow the tone: send it forth easily and freely. . . . Think of your mouth, throat and windpipe as one continuous hollow shaft, the same width as your neck right down to the waist—like the shaft of a well—and think of the AH as starting at the bottom, resounding against the walls, and bursting out at the top.

We want now, to be able to release all the five primary vowels—the basis of our speech—with the same ease and freedom. Yawn again, and instead of "AH" let out a good fat "A . . .!" Mouth and tongue both have to change slightly for the new sound, but the throat arch can remain constant, so can the essential tone-quality. The same applies to the other four vowels. "Yawn-out" each one, matching its fullness and roundness as nearly as possible to the original AH. E and U are the trickiest: one being extra wide and the other extra narrow, the back of the mouth tends to imitate the shape of the front, resulting in a hard E and a pinched U. But with a little experimenting—and *listening*—these two sounds can become just as free and full as the other four.

One being extra wide, the other extra narrow.

Next, yawn-out two vowels in one breath, the first gliding into the second:

AH . . . A . . . /E . . . I . . . /O . . . U . . .

Avoid that little vocal kick in between, known as the glottal stop; it is unnecessary and ugly, and is a sign of throat tension

Release Your Voice and Find Your Personality

—the enemy to free tone. Now try yawning-out three vowels in succession:

AH ... A ... E   I ... O ... U ...

and finally all six sounds, slowly, smoothly and strongly on the one breath.

Aim for one continuous stream of tone, and mentally measure it into six equal parts, so that the last sound is as good as the first. Imagine you are drawing a firm line across a sheet of paper without lifting the pencil, that is, ——————— not — — — — — — keeping the line straight and *uniform in thickness*—that is, not letting the tone droop, or fade.

Take trouble with these simple sounds. They are releasing the fundamental tone upon which all your speech will be built. They are only solid lumps of voice, at the moment, you are like a sculptor working on a slab of shapeless granite, out of which is to be carved something of enduring beauty.

5

Our String Instrument

NOW that we know how to release our natural tones, we need to discover what that tone actually is—and in what numerous ways our control of it can be of help to us, mentally as well as vocally.

We have learnt that voice is created by breath. But how? What exactly *is* voice? We must first ask what sound is, and then we are ready to discover how the brain co-operates with the body to transform mere sound into speech or song.

All sound is vibration. Scientists tell us that everything—all matter, animate and inanimate—is vibration (that, in fact, all matter is living, by virtue of this; a theory too involved for consideration here).

The vibration of air within any narrow space—a chimney, or a keyhole—produces a certain type of note, which varies according to the amount of air, its speed, and the size of the aperture.

An elastic band, when plucked, might be said to produce another type of note, which varies according to the thickness, length and tautness of the band.

A hammer hitting a nail produces yet another type of note, which varies according to the size of the hammer and the composition of the object receiving the nail.

The jet of air, the elastic band, and the hammer, illustrate the three simple principles of vibration governing the three main types of musical instrument, Wind, String and Percussion, and together they represent, crudely, the mechanism of the human instrument—a jet of air projected through a narrow passage, the windpipe, and striking (and vibrating) two flexible bands, the vocal cords.

It is interesting to compare the *methods* of vibration that

Release Your Voice and Find Your Personality

Interesting to compare the methods of vibration.

give various instruments their characteristic Voice. The Hammer family, includes bells, triangle and drums, with only one "vibrator", (and one—or at the most, two—hammers) and piano and zylophone, with rows of parallel vibrators—strings for the one, metal strips for the other. (The piano having a separate little hammer fixed to each of the black or white keys depressed by the fingers.)

The piano is also related to the String family, the most delicate-toned member of which is the harp, its vibrations being caused directly by the fingers—as with all the Guitar group, mandolin, ukulele, banjo, etc.—some say it is this "human touch" that lends to those instruments a specially sentimental appeal.

Piano and harp have dozens of strings. The Violin group have only four each—some of wire, most of catgut—vibrated by the strokes of a bow, unless a special effect called pizzicato, is called

that extra sentimental appeal.

Our String Instrument

Tones of . . . the larger wind instruments
compared
with
the notes of . . . piccolo.

for, when the fingers pluck the strings. The double-bass in modern dance bands is played entirely in this way, to the pain of serious musicians, who call it coffin-thumping.

The vibration of the breath against a single slender reed set in a tubular neck produces the varied tones of oboe, saxophone, and the larger wind instruments, in much the same way as a note is conjured from a blade of grass stretched between the two thumbs, or, simpler still, by the human tongue fluted behind pursed lips. Breath, escaping through parallel holes in a tube, produces the notes of flute and piccolo; manufactured "breath" passing through hundreds of tubes, all lengths and sizes, produces the many toned notes of the grand organ; and *breath passing through a single tube, and vibrating two tiny "strings" of membrame, produces the countless notes of the human voice.*

The vocal cords are set horizontally, side by side, in the larynx or adam's-apple. When we are not talking they lie slightly apart, and the breath passes silently between them, but when we speak they come together, so that the breath strikes and vibrates them.

These cords vary slightly with everyone. They can be long or short, thick or thin, strong or weak, their actual construction being beyond our control; it is one of the factors—but only one—that go to make up the individuality of voices. The whole build of face and feature contributes to this, even the shape of the nose can affect the speech! as we shall shortly discover. If the vocal cords are long (reckoning in minute fractions of an inch) the natural pitch of the voice will tend to lowness, if on the short side it will be correspondingly high.

This rule, that *length affects pitch*, applies to both string and wind instruments. A saxophone is longer than a flute and its notes are considerably lower; visualize the pipes of a grand organ, graduated according to length, each of them producing a sound of different pitch. Note the shape of a grand piano; the left side—housing the lower notes—is considerably longer than the right or treble side, the case being designed to accommodate the varying lengths of the strings. The harp owes its graceful proportions to this fundamental rule of sound.

In the violin and guitar groups, the strings are shortened and lengthened by finger pressure, which means that the player can conjure, from a mere four or six strings, scores of different notes.

The actual note given out by each of the "open" strings (that is, when it is not being stopped by the finger) is further determined by its individual thickness; so are the notes of piano and harp; the taller organ pipes are correspondingly larger in girth: thus we arrive at our second rule—shared by all instruments, including the voice—that *pitch is also affected by thickness*.

Look inside a piano and you will notice that there are three strings to each of the higher notes, in order to match their strength of tone with that of the single lower ones. The piccolo is thinner and lighter than the oboe, so is the sound it produces: which brings us to the third rule of sound—that *thickness affects volume*.

And so we begin to see how the nature of our vocal cords contributes to the difference between one human voice and another, particularly that of the male and female, adult and child.

A woman's Adam's-apple is less prominent than a man's

Our String Instrument

because the cords within are smaller. There is the distance of exactly an octave—that is, eight notes—between the vocal pitch of the two sexes, and their weight of tone differs correspondingly. A child's voice starts life high-pitched and thin (though not necessarily soft!), deepening and strengthening as the cords and larynx develop; whilst in extreme old age, as the cords wear thin and shrink, and the breathing muscles are enfeebled, the tone weakens, and "Turning again towards childish treble, pipes and whistles in his sound".

Incidentally, the so-called "break" in a boy's singing voice, due to the rapid growth of the vocal cords, can largely be eliminated with a little care and common sense. As the range of his voice alters, so should that of the music he is allowed to tackle. None of my choir boys ever needed to drop their singing, they merely omitted the high notes, to begin with, then moved across to the alto benches. One or two stayed there, as valuable male altos, others moved on to join the tenors, some finishing up among the basses.

Returning for a moment to the simile of the wind-in-keyhole; as the speed and force of air increases, so the note gets louder, *and higher*. This seems to suggest that volume is also linked-up with pitch—which would explain why we find ourselves raising our voice when we want it to carry. But a high sound *seems* louder only because it hits the ear more sharply. A low sound, *given the same air pressure*, will carry as far, and more pleasingly, hence the importance of being able to control our breath. Try low *firm* speech on a deaf person, it will be more comfortable for you both and everyone else.

Now we come to the fourth rule of sound—a very significant one for those who seek personal well-being through their speech—that the strength and depth or otherwise of a sound is affected not only by the length and thickness of the vibrating body but also by its *tension*.

Open a piano lid and pluck some of the strings. You'll find the short, thin high ones much tauter than the long, thick low ones. Violinists and cellists need to tune *up*, the strings slacken and their pitch drops through constant bow

Release Your Voice and Find Your Personality

pressure, and the pegs securing them are *tightened* to correct this. A fiddler's E string snaps much more frequently than the lower three, it suffers the most strain because of its extra fineness and tension. The higher the note of a trumpeter, the tighter must his lips be. That delightful muffled pandemonium that pervades a concert platform—with its promise of imminent pleasure—as the orchestra awaits the conductor's tap, comes from everyone testing their tensions.

Similarly, tautness in the vocal cords produces high pitch, slackness produces low. Why do we scream with sudden fright or hurt, and groan with prolonged pain? In the first instance we are physically taut: every muscle is contracted—in instinctive self-defence—psychologists say even the hair stands on end. In the second instance, we have physically let go, through weariness of spirit or exhaustion of body, and in both cases, the vocal cords react in sympathy, *the natural voice expressing—as always—the feelings behind it.*

These are vocal extremes forced on us unwittingly, but some people seem to use them every time they speak, shrilling or rumbling their way through life, straining their voices, and other peoples' nerves, through keeping their cords constantly at one tension. It is like wearing out a stair carpet through never changing the tread, ignoring all the infinite changes that make the human voice the most expressive instrument in the world.

Varied pitch comes instinctively to the released voice, changing in harmony with the changing thoughts and moods of the speaker. The really attractive voice has every kind of change in it, not only pitch but volume, weight (these two are not necessarily the same) speed, timbre—did you know that a voice can actually change colour? These fascinating aspects of speech belong to a later chapter. The point I want to make here is that, just as a melody can be played (or sung) in different keys, according to the range of the particular instrument, so our speech can be melodious on different levels, according to the natural compass of the voice. Few of us use the whole of our compass, and many of us fail to use the *right* compass, which is generally lower than we realize.

Our String Instrument

The higher pitches strike harder on the ear, and are harder on the voice. Prolonged tension of any kind—mental, emotional or physical—is detrimental to well-being, and tension in one department invariably communicates itself to the other two.

HIGH-PITCHED SPEECH IS USUALLY THE OUTWARD EVIDENCE OF SOME SORT OF INNER STRAIN, AND IT IS AN ACTUAL FACT THAT BY WILLING OUR VOICE ON TO A LOWER LEVEL, WE CAN HELP CONSIDERABLY TO LESSEN THAT STRAIN. THE CONSCIOUS USE OF LOW, RELAXED TONE IMPARTS A SENSE OF EASE AND POISE, TRY IT AND SEE!

This does not mean we should *never* introduce the higher notes into our voice. Habitually deep tones—particularly if there is no other kind of variation to relieve them—can be as dull as shrill ones are trying, but the general trend of our conversational tones should, especially among women, be towards depth rather than height, for the comfort of all concerned.

There is another interesting fact about tension in a "vibrating body", that it *affects the number of vibrations, and their speed*.

Strike, and hold down, a top note on the piano and listen... It vibrates so rapidly that the sound vanishes almost as soon as made. Strike a bass note, and its vibrations continue for quite a time, the throbs almost slow enough to be counted. As a matter of interest, notes separated by an octave, above or below, "match" each other because the number of vibrations is exactly halved, or doubled. Harmonies occur when two or more notes are played together whose number of vibrations "fit in". Discord, when odd and even numbers "clash".

Can you see the significance of this—the varying rate of vibrations—as applied to our own speech? It means that any kind of tension speeds up and multiplies our physical vibrations. The heart beats faster, the blood circulates more swiftly, the thoughts race, the words come hurriedly and the voice rises. If, on the other hand, we make a deliberate effort to lower our voice, thus slowing down the vibrations, then the process is reversed: our speech becomes more even, the

Release Your Voice and Find Your Personality

mind calms, the heart steadies, the blood cools, and poise returns.

Of course, the pace at which we talk has nothing *directly* to do with the pace at which our vocal cords *vibrate*, it is just that, when using a lower pitch we tend quite unconsciously to speak more slowly thus giving us time to think.

Rapid speech is a matter of rapid *word sequence*, and is usually the sign of a rapid thinker. But it can also be the sign of an agitated (i.e. tense) thinker—the mind, as usual, giving itself away, via the voice.

The interplay of speed and pitch is expressed in everyday phrases like "hurry *up*", "*high* speed", "*low* vitality", "calm *down*", and is very simply illustrated in the rotating of a gramophone record. The indicator is set at so many revolutions per minute and the motor maintains the required speed, but if the power gives out, the record literally slows *down*, often with ludicrous effect. . . .

Now, it is obvious that *the greater the speed, the greater the power needed to maintain it,* whether for the rotations of a turn-table, or engine wheels, or for the vibrations of a musical sound. A wind-player needs more breath-energy to prolong a high note than a low one, so does a singer (though not necessarily more *breath*). Similarly, *high pitched speech calls for more effort than low*: unnecessary effort, that takes its toll of the speaker, and that could be stored up for more worthwhile use.

This does not mean that energy and forcefulness should be absent from our speech—quite the contrary. Both are necessary if our voice is to help us to "go places", and low pitch is particularly deadly, lacking these qualities (men being the more frequent offenders here). There is a big difference between effortlessness and mere lack of effort. Effort is needed to acquire right breathing, comfortable pitch, pleasing tone, "alive" speech—all the ideals set out in this book. But the effort is chiefly one of concentration. Thinking the right things for the voice, and thinking them continually, in order that our actual *speaking* may be effortless.

This chapter may have seemed to imply, however, that our

Our String Instrument

speech still hangs largely on the sort of voice-box we are born with; that a lot depends on what Nature has given us, and that we have to fight her to get anywhere—men striving to put vitality into voices built to be low and ponderous, women struggling against tones destined to be weak and high, children simply waiting to see what Time will do about it! But whereas the rules of sound are rigid, as applied to mechanical instruments, they merely indicate *tendencies* when applied to the human voice. These tendencies are only a tiny part of the art of speech. We need to know about them in order to co-operate with them, as a craftsman needs to know the nature of his medium. We shall pass on from mere tendencies in the voice to its *possibilities*, and these are infinite.

But first, to sum up what we have learnt about vibration as applied to the human voice. It all boils down to this—that the *basic nature* of the voice is influenced by the length and thickness of the vocal cords, which is not in our hands; and by their tautness, and rate of vibration, which *is*—because our breath controls these vibrations.

And so we return to a subject that has already had two chapters to itself, but now our experiments will be with the breath when transformed into voice.

We know how to steady our breath-stream, with the aid of rib-hold and diaphragm-pressure (symbolized by the cardboard figure and the bell-push!). We now apply these in the same way, to steady our sound-stream.

Inhale a "yawn-full" of air, and instead of the whispered HAH of page 38 *vocalize* it gently, turning the "hand-warming" breath into a stream of warm tone. Don't let it waver—this means the breath is wavering—and carry on only till the lungs are comfortably empty.

Deal similarly with the HISS, which means that it now becomes a Buzz...

Count mentally, and compare the totals with those you reached in the two earlier experiments. But remember there is no need to strive for exceptional totals: *thinned-out breath produces thinned-out tone*.

Did you notice the pitch of your two sound-streams? It

Release Your Voice and Find Your Personality

was probably quite a lot lower than that of your normal conversation: the Natural Voice, released from old habit, choosing its own comfortable, *natural* level.

And now to apply this rib-and-diaphragm control to our yawned vowels. With the same even flow that you achieved—we will assume—on the group of six sounds (p. 48), and at the same easy pitch that your voice chose for that last prolonged BUZZ, yawn them through twice without pause, gliding the "U" of the first group into the "AH" of the second.

Finally—with well expanded "belt"—take the vowels through three times, on one deep yawn-breath.

If you can sustain such a series—smooth, mellow and open-throated throughout—you will prove your command of three essentials—*full breath harnessed to flowing tone and changing sound*—and you will have laid a sure foundation for natural Good Speech.

6

Our Natural Loud Speakers

EVERY sound-maker yields a volume of tone more-or-less in relation to its size. Compare violin and 'cello; the different types of drum; the modern "mini-piano" with the Concert Grand. How is it then, that the two tiny strings of the vocal instrument in their diminutive case—little larger than a Jew's harp—are capable of notes that can fill the Albert Hall, or of words that will make themselves heard above the traffic at Marble Arch?

The answer is, that the Voice Box is not the complete instrument, any more than the keyboard is the complete piano, or the narrow area of string traversed by the bow is the complete violin. The primary sounds of any instrument, human or human-made, are sent ringing through its "body", where they are enlarged and enriched by the process known as Resonance.

Obviously, a thin little body like that of say, the piccolo has room for only a small amount of resonance, whereas the imposing ones of double bass and tuba produce cavernous tones that are the foundation of the whole orchestra. This is not to say that the size of the human body determines the size of its voice—a little man can have a huge voice, and a giant a feeble one. It is the resonators that decide this, according to their shape and build, but most of all according to the use we make of them.

The term Resonance explains itself: "re-sonance"—that is, resound or echo. An echo is produced by a sound rebounding from a hard surface. It can attach itself to the tail-end of the original sound, or there may be an appreciable pause between; the time it takes to respond depending on the distance the sound has to travel, which can vary from a few feet to several miles.

Release Your Voice and Find Your Personality

Echoes are an elusive and fascinating study. There is a mountain range above Grindlewald that gives back a triple echo. A Swiss in picturesque costume produces notes from a giant alpenhorn some fifteen to eighteen feet long, and it is a memorable experience, on that high green slope, to stand in silence *waiting* for the notes to come back, clear on the still air, first from one peak, then, seconds later, from another, and at long last, eerily, as from another world ... A delayed echo has been made the subject of a weird short story (*No Ghosts*, by H. A. Manhood). A corpse is found, still warm, on a bowl-shaped hillside, and the last words of the victim suddenly return and return again—out of nowhere—to betray the killer.

These are long-distance echoes. In musical instruments, and in our own vocal instrument, the echo-area is so close to the source of sound that the echoes amplify the original tone by actually blending with it. But whereas all man-made instruments (except the grand organ) have only one echo-area, and therefore only one quality of tone, Speakers and Singers are provided with a whole series of echo-spots, or resonators, each with its own special effect on the Voice according to its position and size. These resonators are all set in the upper front of the body, from the top of the chest to the top of the head—wherever, in fact, there is a hard inner-surface for the voice to resound against.

No amount of noise will produce any response from soft substances (hence the padded cell). We would not expect to create an echo by shouting into a cushion—the heroine buries her face in one to *smother* her sobs; wheels are fitted with rubber tyres to absorb sound as well as shock. Notice how voices and footsteps ring in an empty house: but as furniture is moved in, so sound is deadened—carpets and curtains and upholstery all help to muffle vibration—till the only place in which ones vocal efforts are heard to advantage is the bathroom! There the shiny surfaces of tile and porcelain and the sound-carrying properties of water all combine to flatter the voice while the impregnability of one's position provides added encouragement.

Our Natural Loud-Speakers

Music studios are generally on the bare side. The serious vocalist never really enjoys performing in a drawing-room, but I have yet to meet one who does not enjoy singing in a church. The stone walls, the smooth pillars, the lofty arched roof all help to enrich his tones. Even the hard pews have their advantage! Some buildings are over resonant, so that the echo from one sound blurs the beginning of the next. Liverpool Cathedral is a modern example: outside, its rose-tinted bricks seem for ever reflecting the sunset, but inside they are for ever reflecting every sound. . . .

The problem of acoustics—and it still is a problem, despite the strides of science—is a study in itself. At present we are concerned, not with the behaviour of the voice in large public buildings, but within its own little private building, the human body, where the simpler rules of reflected sound apply much the same as in any other small enclosed area.

The two essentials for the creation of resonance are hardness and *hollowness*. A wooden floor, or staircase, resounds more than a stone one, because it is hollow. Mentally compare the sound of footfalls as they contact different surfaces—passing first of all through grass, then on to a pathway; next along a tarmac road which leads presently by the side of a high wall; and finally beneath an archway. The resonance increases as the surface becomes more resistant and the area more confined. When the archway is prolonged, as in a railway tunnel, the sounds are continually thrown back on each other, echoing their own echoes.

And so we find that the arch is the ideal shape for resonance. The sounds are completely enclosed, and ring evenly against every part of the surface unable to lurk in crevices, or escape round corners. Our voice is most generously supplied with arches set at five different levels, in the upper chest, the mouth, the nose and cheekbones, the forehead, and the crown

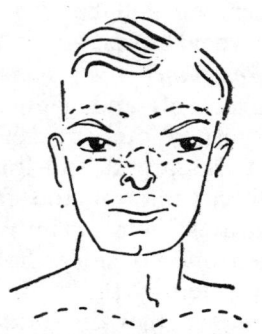

Our voice is . . . supplied with arches.

of the head. As these different arches are brought into action, so the pitch and timbre of the voice varies.

The chest obviously responds to the lowest and heaviest notes; mouth, nose and cheek-bones to the medium ones; forehead and cranium to the highest—though these are seldom called on by the speaking voice except in moments of extreme fright and possibly temper!

Now it can be seen how a person's physique can affect his voice adversely—if he lets it. A narrow chest does not encourage rich, low tones, a large tongue, or crowded teeth can interfere with mouth resonance; small nostrils, or narrow bridge will hamper the voice from ringing freely in the nasal cavities.

Consider the physical build of the negro; large mouth, prominent cheek-bones, wide neck, broad shoulders and chest —all conducive to the full mellow tones that are his birthright; but his nose is short and flat, which may explain why he has difficulty with his nasal sounds (as I have found, in the case of African students).

Although the various arches echo certain sounds more readily than others, *the perfectly produced voice uses all the resonators all the time*, so that the limitations of one cavity may be counterbalanced by greater freedom in another. Thus, a large well-arched roof to the mouth can compensate for say flabby cheeks, and a broad chest for a narrow nose, and so on. In other words, if we make the most of *all* our amplifiers, our tones can still be rich and full, whatever the dimensions of our vocal cords, and whatever the shape of our face!

Resonance does not necessarily mean loudness. A sound can be soft and gentle yet full of resonance. In this sense, the term "loud-speaker" may be misleading, until we realize that the largest and loudest instruments in the orchestra are still capable of the faintest *pianissimo*—their size simply indicates their *capacity* when going all-out. The term is apt when one considers how the tone of radio and gramophone is affected by the quality of its loud-speaker. It is entirely up to us, whether the loud-speakers of our own personal instrument emulate those of the limited portable, the table model or the console de luxe!

Our Natural Loud-Speakers

How do we bring these various natural loudspeakers into play? First of all, of course, by breath control. The largest and most perfectly shaped cavities are useless, unless we have enough breath power to impel our voice into them. It is then a matter of mentally visualizing the different arches in turn, and consciously directing the voice there, aided—to begin with—by certain sounds that feel naturally at home in them, but mainly by an effort of will.

This *willing* of the voice is the real key to the whole art of speech. *We are playing blindfold, on an invisible, intangible instrument* situated in the body, but manipulated by the brain. We cannot put our fingers to it, we can only put our minds to it. That is why some literally "inside" knowledge is essential, if we are to play our instrument effectively.

7

Waking the Echoes

THE mouth is the main resonator, being in the direct vocal route: the quickest way in for the breath and the obvious way out for the voice—straight through into the tool house where tongue, teeth and lips wait to do their job of welding sounds into speech. The mouth forms an echoing tunnel for the voice, culminating in the arch of the hard front palate. Lift your tongue and feel around, and you will realize that it is, in fact, a natural dome—and everyone knows how a dome encourages echo. The acoustic problems of the Albert Hall at once spring to mind. But that which may get out-of-hand in a big space is quite controllable in a small one. The dome of the hard palate is our voice's natural sounding-board, catching and amplifying every sound that passes under it.

I was sauntering with a friend recently, along the terrace of Bexhill's De la Warr Pavilion. As we paused, talking, our voices suddenly altered, sounding huge and hollow, as if we were using megaphones. We stopped in mid-sentence—looked sharply round—but we were alone in an open space facing the open sea. Then I glanced up, and found we had halted directly beneath a small deeply domed cupola. It struck me as a perfect demonstration of what—in miniature—the mouth dome does for our speech.

But only if it is *allowed* to. We must clear the tunnel behind it, first. The vocal tones can be partially lost during their brief journey from the larynx, absorbed by the soft furnishings encountered on the way: the soft palate—if it is allowed to sag; the tongue—unless it lies flat; even the lips—unless they are firmly parted. So again, we realize the importance of the harnessed yawn. Not only does it open the way for bigger breath and freer tone, but also for *natural power*.

Waking the Echoes

Some of the simplest everyday sounds can help us towards better speech. Just as whistling encourages tongue control, so humming encourages mouth resonance.

There are two ways of humming; back in the throat or forward against the lips, right under the mouth dome.

To establish the right way, start with a yawn-breath followed by a soft, prolonged AH, and *during* the AH, close and open the lips gently several times. The effect will be:

ah—mm—ah—mm—ah—mm etc.

Next, to *concentrate* the tone under the mouth dome, repeat the sequence, and at the third MM, continue humming it, gradually increasing the volume till your mouth feels full of sound, and the vibrations set up a tickling sensation against the lips.

Now *start* with the hum, and when the vibrations make themselves felt (not before) open into a single full-blooded AH!

hum, and open into . . . AH!

Try the same thing with each of the other five vowels (still *starting* softly, to ensure there is no forcing)—mmmMMMAY! mmmMMMEE! and so on. Finally, string the six vowels together with a hum linking each, all in the one breath—mmAHmmAmmEmmImmOmmOO! There must be no "daylight" between the sounds, the effect should be of a single stream of growing tone. At the same time we must *avoid intoning*: these recipes are for the speaking—not the singing—voice.

Release Your Voice and Find Your Personality

Our mouth resonance is next applied to words, and then to short sentences. Find words beginning with M followed by each vowel in turn, such as:

MARch, MAjor, MEteor, MIghty, MOat, MOOn.

Choose words as far as possible in keeping with the "important" tone you want to develop. It is easier to give weight and impressiveness to MARvellous than to MARmalade. Then try out some alliterations—"Manners Maketh Man"; "Miles of Marching Men"; etc.

Perhaps you are thinking—what a host of directions for the forming of one little sound.... But the hum is the foundation of vocal resonance, and this last group of experiments is among the most important in the book. They will serve again, slightly adapted, to wake up the echoes in the adjoining hollows—the nasal arches above, and the chest arches below.

Instead of the hummed "M" substitute a hummed "N"—lifting and lowering the tongue instead of opening and closing the lips. Concentrate your thought on the nasal bone (wrinkling the nose seems to help!) till you feel as though something solid is pressing against it.

For N-words you could use:

NARd, NAtion, NEEd, NIght, NOble, NOOn,

and for alliterations: "Now or Never"; "Nine thousand, Nine hundred and Ninety Nine!" Be sure the throat remains open for these: in forming the N-sound the soft palate tends to droop, so that *too much* voice escapes through the nose, producing an unpleasant nasal twang.

There is a vast difference between nasal resonance and nasal *tone*. The nasal echoes, rightly used, simply reinforce those of the mouth dome, and together they lend a most attractive quality to the speaking Voice. Among singers its effect is most noticeable with tenors—who sometimes use it to excess.

The arches of the cheek-bones will ring in sympathy with the nasal arch between them, if its vibrations are sufficiently strong. The cavities of brow and head belong to the higher pitches of the voice, necessary to the singer, and now and then to the actor—if his role demands it—but definitely to be discouraged in everyday speech, if we value popularity.

Waking the Echoes

So we turn, lastly, to the valuable 'cello tone of the chest amplifiers, so often neglected—particularly among women—yet so much easier on the voice as well as on the ear. The virtues of lower speech have already been sung for the acquiring of ease and dignity, but low pitch *alone* is not enough, there must be strength and richness to give it *life*. Our deeper echoes can be awakened by the "G" sound (i.e. as in *Gold*—not the sound of its name, *Gee*). Repeat it several times, placing the fingers at the base of the neck in the "salt cellar" between the collar bones, where a definite bounce can be felt. Now press the palm of the hand flat against the bony "plate" just below, yawn-breathe, and utter a deep, prolonged "GAH...!" You will feel its vibration like bees buzzing in your chest.

Put "G" before the other five vowels in turn:
  Gay...! Gee...! Gi...! Go...! Goo...!
Now link three smooth vowels to one "G":
  Gah...ay...ee...! Gi...o...oo...!
Then make one mighty "G" do for the lot:
  Gah—a—e—i—o—oo!
(making sure the tone remains deep and strong till the end of the "oo").

Pass on to words and alliterations:
  GUARd, GAme, GEEse, GUIde, GOAl, GOOn.
  Go, Get you Gone! A Good Game of Golf.

The secret of chest resonance is relaxation. The vocal cords slacken as the pitch descends, and the whole area around them should relax in sympathy. If you "dig" at your deep sounds—chin tucked into collar, jaw rigid, shoulders hunched—the tone will be hard and rasping. Hold your head level, even tilt the chin slightly (not too much), and imagine your words are dead weights being dropped straight down a hollow shaft—your throat—into the depths of a well....

Having achieved resonance on sounds that naturally belong in the mouth, nose and chest, we must next be able to set these echo-spots ringing *without* the help of M, N and G.

Find sentences that seem to you appropriate to the pitch and tone-quality of each. For instance:
  CHEST—Woe to the false Etruscan...

Release Your Voice and Find Your Personality

MOUTH—Life is real—life is earnest!
NOSE (and CHEEKS)—Lift up your heads, O ye gates.
And just for the sake of experiment (only!):
FOREHEAD—Over the mountains and over the waves.
TOP OF HEAD—Shrieking and squeaking in fifty different sharps and flats!

Try moving from one amplifier to another in the course of one sentence:

UPWARDS—And hamlets brown, and dim discovered spires.
DOWNWARDS—So smiles the day star in the ocean bed.

All the above, of course, will sound somewhat exaggerated and artificial. It is bound to. We are doing a somewhat exaggerated and artificial thing, in trying to *isolate* our echoes—the final step is to blend them, releasing the *whole* of our natural voice in all its new-found richness. You will need some fine, resounding phrases. Shakespeare is master of them:

O what a rogue and peasant slave am I!
Time's glory is to calm contending Kings.
Rome, thou hast lost the breed of noble bloods.

If you feel more at home with prose, declaim some headlines from the day's newspaper:

ASTOUNDING VALUE IN NEW SEASON'S FURS.
KNIFE ATTACKER GETS FIVE YEARS.
300,000 WENT TO THE PROMS.

Follow this up with longer passages, a dramatic item of news, or a colourful paragraph from a book.

Once the voice has learnt to release its full power, it is as well to try out the resonators on gentler speech. We have no wish to develop penetrating tones that force themselves upon everyone within earshot. Resonance, as I have said, is not *necessarily* loudness, any more than the right-foot piano pedal is the "loud" pedal, though it is often referred to as such. Notice how any good pianist uses this "*sustaining*" pedal continually, even in *pianissimo* passages—it lifts the velvet dampers from the strings, so as to release their full vibration: and this, in effect, is what Resonance does for our vocal strings. It increases not so much the volume as the cubic-content of the voice, so that the softest tones need never be *weak* ones.

Invent some more alliterations, this time of a suitably subdued nature, and dwell on the initials but keep the vowel tone under:

>Mmysterious, Mmagical Mmusic . . .
>Nnameless and Nnebulous . . .
>Graceful, Ghostly Galleons Gliding.

Then read aloud an eerie passage from a thriller or a ghost story!

But remember, to develop full resonance you *must* go all out, at first, or you will never discover the latent possibilities of your instrument. Release everything you've got. Where is the sense in being shy with yourself? You must have enough material to work on, just as a sculptor needs a block of stone much larger than the delicate shape that presently will emerge. . . . If you cannot get alone in a field, or alone in the house, issue a warning to those whom it may concern—lock your door—and steel yourself against "feeling silly". You are only practising your instrument as others practise singing or the piano. Open the throat, open the ribs and use *all your breath on all your tone*—you are developing moral as well as vocal courage.

8

The Shape of Words to Come

THE human voice is the only sound-maker that can change shape for every sound it makes. Except, of course, the ones created by Walt Disney. In his inspired cartoons, trumpets and hooters and engine-funnels swell or elongate or shrink in accordance with the noises emitted. . . . Every normal musical instrument has the one characteristic shape by which it can be recognized, and should it not be visible —on sound radio, or hidden in an orchestra—then we know it by its "voice"—which has only one characteristic tone.

But the Human Instrument has many shapes and innumerable tones. We can alter its timbre or "colour" at will and we can alter its shape—at the bellows-end, when we breathe, and at the business-end, when we speak.

The typical child's drawing of a human face makes the mouth a slit, and that is how most of us think of it. True, it tends towards this shape *in repose*, due to the formation of the grinning skull behind it. Nature planned every unit of our frame with an unerring sense of fitness-for-purpose, and the purpose of the jaw being primarily, to open and close over nourishment, we cannot deny the suitability of its design—mastication would be somewhat difficult if the mouth was fixed vertically on the face, though it would be an asset to vocal tone (as may be gathered from the mouthings of some dramatic singers).

Nature apparently decided that taking in food is more important than letting out sound, so she gave us the wide jaw. But she also gave us facial muscles,

The mouthings of some dramatic singers.

The Shape of Words to Come

with which it is possible to counteract not only this "fixed grin" but any other personal mouth trend that might be detrimental to our speech. The mouth need not keep to the shape it was born with. It is essential that it shouldn't if the sounds we utter are to have any character or variety.

Sound, like liquid, *takes on the shape of the hole through which it exits.* Pour water from a kettle—its form is narrow and tubular; from a jug—it becomes fluted; a basin—and it will be wide and flat. Similarly, sound is shaped by the formation of the lips, so the type of mouth we happen to possess must, obviously, have some effect on the tones that come out of it: and once again we see how physical tendencies can react upon the voice.

A thin mouth is likely to produce a thin voice—pinched and precise, if the lips tend to the pursed position; flat-toned and metallic if they are inclined to spread wide. We would not expect a person described as "tight-lipped" to possess mellow tones. We'd suspect him of a hard nature—with voice to match. Flabby lips frequently go with slovenly speech—and a slovenly mind: for mental tendencies, also, react upon the voice.

An actor makes up his mouth to suit his part—narrow, full, drooping, smiling—according to the character to be portrayed, and when he speaks he *uses his lips* correspondingly, so that his voice is in character, too. If, then, a voice can be adapted to "match" the mouth, it can also be adapted to counteract it, should this be desirable. A small mouth need not *necessarily* mean a small voice *or* a small mind—we can learn to enlarge all three—if we recognize these tendencies and are ready to face up to them.

Besides, the mouth is not the only facial feature that influences tone, as we have already discovered. Every face has its compensations! Thin lips may have a beautiful dome behind them, a small mouth may partner a large nasal arch, and so on. So that, with a little knowledge and imagination, we can find out how to make the most of our good points, and how to combat others.

We know how to release our voice and how to develop its tone; we come, now, to the shaping of that tone.

Release Your Voice and Find Your Personality

Many people have completely shapeless speech. Their upper lips are rigid—apparently glued to the top teeth—and their lower lips just flap up and down, letting out blobs of sound that are characterless and boring. English people, especially the Southerners, are notoriously guilty here. The British Bull-dog Jaw and the Stiff Upper Lip may indicate hardness of character: they certainly produce hardness—and drabness—of tone; and they usually have a similar effect on the rest of the face! Immobile lips mean drooped cheek muscles, which seem to dull the expression of the eyes, whereas mobile lips give animation and interest to both face and voice.

It may be argued that some people—including professional speakers and actors—seem scarcely to move their lips, yet every sound is full and clear, and every look expressive. The answer is, that these individuals have extra control over their facial muscles, and if one "set" is inactive, it simply means that more work is going on elsewhere: if the mouth is practically closed against the tone, the resonators have to be doubly responsive; if the lips are lazy, the tongue has to be twice as energetic. Slackness in one department demands overtime in another.

Prove this to yourself. Repeat rapidly our six basic vowels—first, with exaggerated mouth movement; then with rigid jaw. In the first case the tongue will seem scarcely to move—the mouth is doing all the work; in the second, you will find the tongue surprisingly acrobatic—and you will have learnt the main secret of the ventriloquist. He can speak clearly and loudly through a mouth that is absolutely still, because he has trained his tongue—in conjunction with teeth and mouth roof—to take over all the sounds normally made by the two lips (also because he has developed tremendous facial—particularly nasal-resonance). This sort of speech is bound to suffer some distortion, so he gives his dummy an exaggerated "character" voice, which serves the double purpose of contrasting completely with his own, and camouflaging imperfections.

But our aim as ordinary people using speech in ordinary

The Shape of Words to Come

spheres, is equal distribution of labour, each section of our instrument doing its own particular job efficiently.

The jobs that are done *inside* the Mouth—by tongue, teeth, and roof—we will leave for a later chapter, when we come to the forming of words. The final step in the forming of *tone* is control of the mouth itself—the hole through which our tone must pass in order to reach our hearers.

Poor mouth movement has the effect of neutralizing all the vowel-sounds, reducing each one to a muddy "er", which results in sentences such as:

"Erv gert ter gert herm ert herf-perst wern."

"Sher's gerng erp ter Merncherster termerrer."

People who speak indistinctly are sometimes advised to open their mouths wider. This certainly helps to let out more sound, but does little to help its *clarity*. The mouth may use *bigger* movements, but if they are all the same *kind* of movement then the Voice will still have only one kind of tone. The mouth frames the speech, and by changing the shape of the frame we can change the shape of the sounds that pass through it, so that each has a separate "character" of its own.

The mouth moves in three directions—sideways, forwards and downwards—the first two by means of the lips, the third by means of the jaw. Obviously the muscles involved need exercise, if they are to do their job efficiently—just as one needs to exercise the finger muscles for dexterity at the piano, or the arm and leg muscles for dexterity in sport.

First, by way of lip drill, pout the lips as far forward as you can push them, then see how widely you can grin. . . . Do this several times, quickly, on the sounds "oo-ee".

Now repeat "see to me—do me too" in a whisper. Whispering enables one to concentrate on movement without the distraction of sound.

Next, to "oil" the hinges of the jaw. These can be located by the small round bone just in front of each ear. Find them with the finger tips, then drop the jaw, and you will feel the bone move forward and downward, whilst the finger slips up and back into the resulting cavity . . . If your jaw cracks,

Release Your Voice and Find Your Personality

you'll know it hasn't been getting enough exercise when you speak. You can see these "hinges" at work if you watch someone, in profile, enjoying a meal.

How deeply can you "gape" your jaw? Wag it up and down several times quickly; jerk it from side to side; thrust it forward and back, bringing the lower teeth in front of the upper. These last two movements may not be associated with any particular speech sound, but they help flexibility—especially of facial expression.

Now do the following in a rapid whisper, three times each:
(*a*) Gape and pout, repeating "ah-oo".
(*b*) Gape and grin—"ah-ee".
(*c*) Pout and gape—pout and grin, on the words "you are, you see—you see, you are".

After which your mouth will probably feel like a strip of much-stretched elastic. . . .

The next step is to apply these mouth shapes to our six main vowels.

Say them slowly, watching your mouth in a mirror. It should change thus—

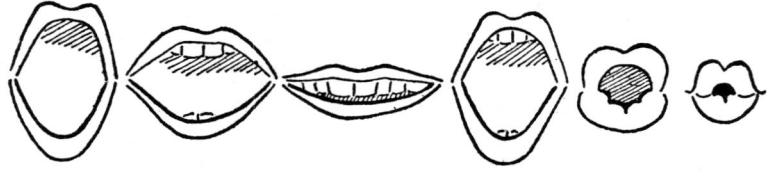

Your mouth should change shape thus—

—moving from tall to wide for the first three and from tall to forward for the other three. Don't forget to use the upper lip as well as the lower. Both lips should move freely, *independent of the teeth*, so that the front teeth top and bottom are visible for at least three of the six sounds, as above.

If your upper lip is lazy, try lifting and relaxing it vigorously, like a dog baring its teeth. Now whisper these two sentences, first slowly, then quickly:

The Shape of Words to Come
PA GAVE ME MY OWN TOOLS
YOU KNOW MY NIECE PLAYS CARDS

still using a mirror, in case the mouth becomes lazy when it has words to negotiate.

Finally, whisper odd proverbs to yourself, deciding which of the main words tend towards a pout, a grin or a gape.

For example *"Look* be*fore* you *leap"* would be—pout, gape, grin; and "A *roll*ing *st*o*ne gath*ers no *moss"* pout, pout, grin, gape.

There is no need to reshape every part of every word—the result would be absurdly pedantic. Some people attempt to do this when reading aloud in public, under the impression that they are speaking extra clearly. Actually they are *less* clear, in that they are completely destroying the natural rhythm of the language.

So, avoid overdoing it: a mouther is as tiresome as a mutterer. And do not worry unduly as to which shape is best for a word. "Safety first" can be equally clear as, grin, gape or, gape, pout. The important thing is that your words *are* shaped, instead of sliding out, dull and undistinguished, from a faintly wagging slit! Shapely speech can be as pleasing as a shapely figure—or nose—or ankle. . . .

Keep in mind the general rule that any word that *can* be spoken—without distortion—with a dropped jaw should be so treated: simply because the common tendency is not to drop the jaw enough. Whisper this one sentence to yourself once a day: *"Does my chin wag when I chin-wag?"* at the same time suiting the action to the question.

To complete our tone-shaping, we ought now to review the rest of the English vowel sounds. A grasp of these, besides helping towards clearer speech, will serve as a check-up on our pronunciation.

Not everyone realizes that the five vowels of the alphabet represent at least seventeen different "noises". Our yawned "Ah", for instance, is one of the sounds belonging to the letter A, as in *half-past*. But Northerners and Americans flatten this sound, making it the same as in *hat*. There are

Release Your Voice and Find Your Personality

some affected individuals who half-swallow it—*hawf pawst*; and others who clip it—*huff pust*. But we will leave these considerations to a separate chapter, making it easier to return to—or to skip—according to your interest in this vexed, but intriguing subject.

9

Speaking and Listening

OUR Pronunciation depends largely on how we shape our vowels. Certain consonants are also involved, such as R, which some people *twans*form into a W, and to which the Scot gives such a beautiful b*r*isk t*r*ill; T, which some people replace by a *sor'* of grunt, and which the Irish lisp so attractively; and L, which some peo*poo* seem to swallow, and which, doubled, the Welsh make so delicate and elusive . . . These are three clear examples of the difference between wrong and *regional* speech—but consonants belong to another chapter.

There is a standard sound for each vowel, and for "standard" the English take Central London (*not* Oxford!) as the French take Parisian, and the Germans Berliner Doitch; but again, there are all manner of deviations from these, embracing the accents of different countries (speaking the same basic language) and the dialects of different counties—or provinces—which vary again from district to district, especially in the more isolated rural areas, where less influence enters from outside.

But Pronunciation is too vast a subject for more than the briefest reference here. There is only space to indicate the generally accepted sounds in speech, and a few of the more obvious "lapses", so that the reader can compare these with his own, and get some idea as to where and how they differ from Standard English.

First, a few remarks about the first letter of the Alphabet, A.

If you say it very slowly you will find you are actually making two different sounds, one merging into the other: *eh* as in *be*d) gliding into *ih* (as in *bi*d). And this leads us to further discoveries—an alternative sound for both E and I.

Listen to A, "eh-ih", again. The two sounds are not of equal length. Which is the longer one? In other words, do

Release Your Voice and Find Your Personality

you say tray as "TREH-ih" or "treh-EEE"? (There is only one "double vowel" that has a longer *second* sound: can you identify it?)

It may be that your pronunciation of the A sound does not include either *eh* or *ih*. The Cockney turns it into an I, and for *May Day*, says *M'y D'y*. The Aust*ry*lian is inclined to do the same but without the nasal twang. The Scotsman uses only the second part of the diphthong, making it *Mee Dee*. The refeened type uses only the first part—*Meh Deh*. I've heard it drawled so as to become *Mer-ih Der-ih*, and crooned through a microphone as *Meh-eeeeee Deh-eeeeeee* ...

Does your own version fit any of these? If not, exactly what sound *do* you make in words containing this "long" A, as it is called?

Of the above variations, the first three are quite acceptable, *in their own locality*—that is where they belong—but the other three are needless distortions. There is a world of difference between mis-shapen speech and Regional Speech. The latter has an attraction of its own—it gives vitality and character to the language. It is a part of our national history. No one need be diffident about possessing a dialect—provided he speaks it intelligibly.

It will be recalled that our language contains at least seventeen vowels. Some experts claim that there are many more. It takes a delicate ear to single out more than twenty. I have purposely narrowed them down to the minimum that the average speaker needs to recognize.

To begin with, each of the five "long" vowels has a short form.

Compare—BĀTE, BĒĒT, BĪTE, BŌAT, BŪDE
with—băt, bĕt, bĭt, bŏttle, bŭd.

There is also the double O, both long and short, as in Bōō̄t and Bŏok, bring the number up to twelve. Repeat the above in pairs, Bāte-Băt, Bēēt-Bĕt, etc., with good lip and jaw movements and you will find that each vowel can change shape for its short sound.

I say *can* change, because *all* the words could also be spoken with exactly the same feeble wag throughout! But if our aim

Speaking and Listening

is Personality Through Speech, that is hardly the way to encourage it. Refer to a mirror, to ensure that your mouth *does* change. Its movements always feel much more exaggerated than they look. . . .

Once we have grasped the difference between the long and short vowels, we can quickly detect when people change them around, as when sōōn becomes *sŏon*, (and sōup—*sŏop!*) when gĕt is *gĭt* and a hăt is a *hĕt*; or when *bŭlb* and *bōld* are both given the same treatment, becoming *bŏl-b* and *bŏl-d*. . . .

But the short vowels are easy to correct, in that they consist of one unchanging sound (called a monophthong) whereas all save one of the long vowels are double sounds, or diphthongs—that is, one sound gliding into another. (Can you find the exception?)

The interesting thing is that no one ever goes wrong on the second sound of the pair (except perhaps to over-prolong it). Say each long vowel very slowly, and you shouldn't find it difficult to detect that the second sound both in A and I is *ih* and the second one in O and U is *oo*, but the first sounds are much less obvious to the untrained ear. Can you identify them?

Because so many faults in pronunciation occur with these five Alphabet vowels, I offer the following "rhyme" for repeating aloud—on the principle that to say a wrong sound deliberately, in conjunction with the right one, helps to distinguish the two:

    A sounds like Ĕ-ĭ, not AH-ĭ
        So a Tray is not a "Try"

    E is just E, not er-ee
        So a Tree is not a "Trer-ee"

    I sounds like AH-ĭ, not AW-ĭ
        So a Tie is not a "Toy".

    O sounds like er-oo, not ă-oo
        So a Toe is not a "Tă-oo"

      •   •   •

Release Your Voice and Find Your Personality

U sounds like ĭ-oo not oo
So the News is not the "Noos"

These are only the most obvious mispronunciations—you might like to add to the list—but to give some idea of the numerous variations possible, here are eighteen versions of O, as heard in that much-used word No:

Nah, Nah-oo, Nă, Nă-oo, Naw-oo, Nay, Neh, Neh-oo, Ner, New, Nŏ-ooo, Noh-oooo, Noo, Now, Nuh, Nuh-oo, Nix and Nope!

Its opposite number, YES, has as many variants (if not more). I have heard:

Yah, Yahss, Yass, Yayss, Yeh, Yeah, Yees, Yerss, Yez, Yerz, Yep, Yip, Yiss, Yuh, Yup, Yuss, mm and uh-huh!

—not to mention "Sure", "You've said it" and the interminable "That's right" . . .

Returning to our seventeen standard sounds. Of the remaining five, we have already met with three—AH, AW and ER (as in *bath*, *ball* and *Bert*).

Er was noted as the first half of the diphthong O. This busy little sound can be represented by every one of the five vowels, as in the sentence:

"*E*arly b*i*rds des*e*rve *a* f*u*rry w*o*rm".

No wonder some people—and not only foreigners—have difficulty with their English spelling!

A whole chapter could be devoted to the use and mis-use of this "neutral vowel" as it is called. I would only urge you not to over-use it as a lazy substitute for other sounds (as in the two dreary sentences on p. 73 of the previous chapter) and not to let *ah* take its place—under the mistaken impression that you sound cultured. I assur-ah you it will nevah impress anyone who re-ahly mattahs!

Finally, AH and AW give us two further diphthongs:
AH gliding to oo as in Bout
AW „   „ ĭ „ „ Boil

Incidentally, there are differences of opinion as to the precise ingredients of diphthongs. I give what I have personally found to be the simplest. The thing to remember is that the two

Speaking and Listening

parts are not equally stressed, except in O. The second half of A, I, OW and OY is very light, the second half of U is dwelt on. We speak of a "bright new coin" as a BRAH-ĭt nĭ-OO CAW-in, not a brah-EEt NEEoo cawEEN.
The most ill-treated of the six diphthongs is OW. The Classic query "How now brown cow?" suffers many strange renderings. Go through the following list aloud—horizontally, then vertically:

hă-oo	năoo	brăoon	căoo
har	nar	brahn	car
heh-oo	něoo	brěoon	cěoo
heh	neh	bren	ceh
hew	new	brewn	cew
hoo	noo	broon	coo
huh-oo	nŭ-oo	brŭ-oon	cŭ-oo

Do you recognize any of these versions as your own? And can you distinguish the dialects from the diabolicals? (They include Sussex, Scots, Oxford and Kensington).

To sum-up (before this chapter turns into an examination paper) all the main vowels of Standard English are contained in the following "rhyme":

A—E—I—O—U
Man gets in hot tub look!
Hark, call the cows, Boy Blue.

Note that "the" is heard as *ther* before a consonant, and *thee* before a vowel—one of the many rules that we all keep without knowing it.

If any particular vowel-sound gives you trouble, search out—or invent—simple phrases on the lines of the Cow Question, as:

Hark, hark the lark.
The dame has a lame, tame crane.
Three, green beech trees.
Mum's currant bun is underdone.

and so on.

The art of correct speaking is fifty per cent the art of correct *listening*—to ourselves, and to others. Listen to the vowels

Release Your Voice and Find Your Personality

around you. Watch the mouths of those who utter them—decide if their shapes are helping or hindering the sounds that emerge, and whether those sounds are Standard, Regional, dead wrong or merely lazy.... You need never be bored on a railway journey: you can mentally be imitating the speech of your fellow-travellers—the bad as well as the good—and you will soon be able to detect *exactly* what changeover is taking place when you overhear talk of (say) Coop Ties; grundstunds (or grend-stends); blew-prints; carfee (or cawfee or cuffee); and fellers and gals (or gels or goils)!

Hence the label "lah-de-dah".

The essential condition for good speech is that it should be pleasing—every other quality is measured by that yardstick, and the two extremes of unpleasing speech are slovenly and illiterate at one end of the scale, exaggerated and mannered at the other—the "varsity type", that overworks the "AH" sound, making every possible vowel a tall one (hence the label "lah-de-dah"), and the refeened type that flattens them all.

How would you prefer to be greeted:
"Hah-yah? Larvleh weathah...."
"Hoo-dee-dew? Nace deh, eesn't eet?" or
"Hellaow! Enit lavloy?"
Of this choice of evils I hope you'd choose the third. At least it is downright and unpretentious.

Good speech does not draw attention to itself in any way —it is natural, unexaggerated, and completely *normal*.

The late King George V taught me this. I think I can claim it was he who gave me my first Elocution lesson.

As a child I had no particular interest in Speech as such, but I had never heard a Royal Voice—it was then the Cat's-whisker stage of Radio—and I was looking forward with eager expectancy to one of the King's early broadcasts. I believe it was to mark his recovery from the illness from which he convalesced at Bognor Regis—giving the town its proud suffix. Loud-speakers had been set up in the main

Speaking and Listening

thoroughfares, and I stood in the waiting crowd anticipating something after the style of Henry V before Agincourt. ... When those modest measured tones began, I turned to my father in astonishment and whispered "Is *that* the King? But he doesn't sound a bit posh!"

I learnt, then, that to speak really well one must use—quite literally—the King's English. It is the Queen's English as I write: and his grand-daughter has the same unassuming, yet confident charm of voice and manner.

10

Mumbling — and Why

WHEN we say someone's voice is "a pleasure to listen to" what *exactly* do we mean?
That it is pleasing in tone? View's vary as to what sort of tone *is* pleasing. We may admire the cavernous Orson Welles or Martita Hunt type of voice, or the mellow, measured Churchillian style, or the lovable lilt of Audrey Hepburn, or the cool, bright tones of the Queen. But there is one quality essential to a pleasing voice, whatever it's weight or pitch, and that is—clarity. Lacking this, no speaker or actor can possibly be considered top rank. Some of our younger players need reminding of this. Singers have sometimes got away with it—or rather without it—chiefly because there is always the music to hold their hearers' interest. And yet, it was almost certainly the words that originally inspired the song.

The Mumbler is a tiresome person, and a stupid one, asking to be ignored. People only half listen if they can only half hear—whereas crystal clear utterance at once attracts interest, possibly because it is so rare.

Haven't you heard a group of people chattering together, arguing some point—interrupting each other—and suddenly a clear (not necessarily loud) voice cuts in, and everyone stops short and listens attentively? What that voice has to say may not be momentous—its owner may have less to give than some of the chatterers—but he gets a hearing, and his words carry weight simply because of the way he utters them.

Fine diction is a delight to the ear, and no one can deny its advantage in business and social life: it helps us to stand out from the crowd for the simplest of reasons—that if people find it *easy* to listen to us they are willing to give us their attention.

Mumbling—and Why

Mumbling sometimes comes from *lack of confidence*. We feel we have nothing of value to say, so we take no pride in the saying of it. In that case, why say it at all? It will probably pass unnoticed, anyway; whereas, by keeping quiet, at least we won't say something we might afterwards regret. We may even give the impression of wisdom—simply because we don't happen to have said anything foolish. And while we are silent we can be sorting out our thoughts, so that when we do open our mouths we produce something that we feel is worthy of clear utterance.

Some of us speak carelessly through *thinking carelessly*, blurting out whatever comes into our head without troubling what words we use or how we utter them. If only we would make the effort to speak more deliberately (and it *is* an effort, if we're not made that way) we would actually find ourselves thinking more deliberately, partly because we would be giving ourselves more *time* to do so, and partly because—subconsciously—we would become aware of the need to choose better words to match our better speech—silly things said carefully sound so *very* silly!

Often our speech would be clear enough if only we talked less *rapidly*. The tongue and lips just haven't time to make all the movements necessary. This may be the result of nerves or it may simply be that our quick speech comes from a quick brain. The mind races ahead of the voice and the words tumble out, only half articulated, in their effort to keep up with our over-eager ideas. Quick thought is obviously an asset that no one would wish to curb, provided it is also *clear* thought; and the same applies to the speech that expresses it!

Many of us—particularly if we are Southern English—don't give our speech muscles *room to move*. If the jaw is held rigid the space inside the mouth is so limited that the tongue and lips are cramped and hampered. A hammer needs swing-space, so does the tongue-tip. . . .

But there are many mumblers who can blame none of these things. They talk quite slowly and thoughtfully, they are neither shy nor tense, but their speech movements are vague

Release Your Voice and Find Your Personality

and sluggish simply because they have no idea which muscles are involved, or what those muscles should be doing.

It is astonishing how ignorant the average person is about what goes on inside his own mouth. I have had a roomful of thoroughly intelligent adults clicking and grunting over their G's and Q's and Y's completely bewildered by the complexity of sounds they have been uttering—or semi-uttering—the whole of their lives.

This is the sort of dialogue that takes place:

ME: Who can describe how to make the "J" sound?
    (Chorus of *JAYS* and *JERS* and ch-ch-ch's)
ME: Stop playing trains and tell me.
VOICE 1: You sort of hiss.
ME: How do you hiss?
VOICE 2: Well, it's more of a buzzy-puff, really.
ME: Yes, but how do you *do* it?
VOICE 3: You purse your lips and push.
ME: Push what?
VOICE 4: No you don't. It's your tongue.
    (Chorus of enlightened "yesses"!)
ME: What do you do with your tongue?
    (Silence. More train noises.)
  Well?
VOICE 5: You blow over the top of it.
ME: All right. Blow over the tops of your tongue, everybody. (A rushing mighty wind ensues.) Is that a J?
EVERYBODY (dejectedly): No....
ME: What *do* you do with your tongue, then?
VOICE 6: Well you do something with your voice as well.
ME: Yes. *What!*
    (Further chorus of JAYS and JERS and ch-ch-ch's.)
ME: Stop playing trains....
and so on.

It's absurd of course. Absurd that such ignorance should exist. That people should be content to go about making hundreds of complicated noises without the least conception of how they are doing it.

Actually, it is rather amazing that any of us *can* talk clearly,

Mumbling—and Why

when one considers the haphazard way in which, as children, we were allowed to pick up the art of speech. (As though any Art can be casually "picked up"!) At home we were encouraged to imitate words; at school we were taught to pronounce and spell them; but never were we given any guidance as to the physical processes involved: these were left to chance.

But it is these physical processes that are the very foundation of language, as we soon realize if we consider the natural stages by which the average child acquires his native tongue.

At first he relies entirely on vowel sounds—AH! and ER! mostly—interpreted by eloquent facial-expression and violent —if vague—gesture.

Presently he discovers that he has in his possession a whole set of new toys—a Tongue that can click, a Throat that can grunt, a Mouth that can make popping and humming sounds. All day he is experimenting with these fascinating noises; and, when several of them together produce something resembling a word—whatever he happens to be looking at, at that particular moment, is identified with it. For instance, one of the first movements he discovers—because it is the simplest —is to wag his jaw so that his tongue taps against his gums: "Da-da-da-da" is the sound it makes—as he lies in Mother's arms, gazing at Father. . . . Another easy movement is to press and open his lips—"Mum-mum-mum"—and so Mother gets her nick-name, too.

Every child has pet noises that only the family understands, and parents comparing notes have discovered that some of these "words" are being used by other children, though the meaning attached to them is entirely different. Popping the lips and bouncing the back of the tongue are movements that every infant discovers long before he knows what words to use them for, and so he combines them in ways of his own. My little nephew was gazing at a large apple when he suddenly exclaimed "*Booka!*" But a friend's child discovered the same "word" when grabbing at his father's bunch of keys. "Gugga" has always meant horse in my family—it probably has countless translations among other small children.

Release Your Voice and Find Your Personality

Whilst the child is experimenting with his speech-toys, he is also becoming aware of the words being used around him, and soon feels the urge to mimic them. Naturally his ear is untrained and his speech muscles unpractised, and he produces some quaint variations. He loves sugar, and wants to ask for it, but *sh* and *g* are too complicated to tackle, so close together. He gets the first *vowel*, however—the stressed one—and he copies the lilt of the word (all children respond quickly to rhythm) and the result is "*oo*-oo".

His ear is always quicker at recognizing new sounds than his tongue and lips are at producing them, and though he isn't sure what muscles to use he gets the effect quite cleverly. The tongue finds it easy to tap the teeth—not so easy to tuck itself between them, so *th*is and *th*at becomes *d*is and *d*at. He is cute enough to hear that some *th*'s have more puff in them than others and for *th*ink he says *f*ink.

Again, the tongue enjoys flicking against the roof of the mouth, but boggles at having to vibrate, so ve*r*y becomes ve*ll*y; or the tongue may be scared off the job completely, and the lips take over instead, making it ve*w*y—a substitution that sometimes persists beyond childhood.

The vibration of the tongue-tip is quite an intricate operation, and the wonder is, not that a few people find it difficult, but that so many find it simple.

S is another tricky tongue-sound. It is not really surprising that the fluting of the blade, and the delicate control of the tiny jet of air that must pass along it, occasionally baffles a youthful speaker, resulting in various forms of lisp.

Most of us outgrow our early speech problems. Some shirk the effort of mastering them, and carry their small errors into adult life; a few are incapable of making the exact movement needed owing to some slight defect, such as a thick tongue that won't "tip", or a frenum (its under-ligament) that is too short, or ill-placed, or just not there.

Occasionally *lack of ear* is the cause of the trouble. Certain sounds do not fully "register" and so are wrongly reproduced.

I have no space to enlarge on these aspects of the subject.

Mumbling—and Why

In any case the personal advice of a speech therapist will achieve more than chapters of words.

R and S are the only two consonants that present any muscular difficulty, all the others are dead easy. They are not so much *mis*-pronounced as insufficiently pronounced, or not pronounced at all—partly through carelessness, but mostly, as I have said, through plain ignorance regarding the whole process of articulation.

11

Our Percussion Instrument

THERE are only two kinds of "noise" we can make, just as there are only two kinds of sign we can write—Vowels and Consonants.

The Vowels are, so to speak, the body of our speech, the Consonants are the bone and muscle that hold the flesh together. To return to our use of musical similes—not all the instruments in an orchestra are capable of playing tunes; some have no tone at all—their purpose is solely to provide rhythm and attack. Similarly, in the miniature orchestra of the human voice, there are sounds that sing and flow and sounds that tap and beat.

Consonants are to speech what rhythm is to melody. A tune would be characterless if it just streamed on and on without the vigour and impetus of recurring stresses—and the stronger those stresses, the more vigorous the tune.

It is the percussion instruments that supply the "highlights", setting off the sonorous flow of strings and reeds. Imagine a Spanish dance without castinets; a Wagner overture without drums: our own serene National Anthem is enormously enhanced by that isolated cymbal-clash which heralds the final phrase (and which always sends a little thrill of patriotism up my spine)—it is like a sudden tongue of flame setting triumphant fire to that unassuming melody. . . .

Consonants give words their individuality. If there were no vowels between, the meaning would still be distinguishable. Witness the typical "small ad". Hieroglyphics like:

"Frnshd Flt, slf cntnd; 3 bd., 2r, ktch., bth."

convey all the necessary information. But strip words of their consonants, and the sense disappears. Who would recognize even the first two words of the above announcement

Our Percussion Instrument

if abbreviated to "u-i a"? Yet that is much the sort of effect produced by some people's speech!

I recently overheard this sentence, as two men passed me in the street:

"I davim ri er ou er le'er"

—which I judged to mean that someone should be asked to write a letter for someone. . . . Need I add that the speaker's overcoat was flapping open (with sleeves a couple of inches too long) and that his shoes—and his hair—could have done with a brush? Laziness in speech is generally a sign of laziness in other directions. The appearance of that particular man had nothing to do with poverty: it costs nothing to turn up a hem or wield a brush.

Poorness is sometimes another word for laziness, and poorness of speech undoubtedly is *laziness: every voice is a good voice— but we have to bestir ourselves in order to prove it so. Poor speech is not the prerogative of poor people: there are as many classes of bad speaking as there are of bad manners, and indistinct speech* is *bad manners: it implies lack of consideration for those to whom we talk.*

Clear speech, then, depends not only upon shaped vowels but upon crisp consonants, and these—as will have been gathered from our brief analysis of baby-talk—depend largely upon the movements of tongue and lips, leaving a few to be shared with the teeth—when they arrive.

There are only five of these basic movements—one for the lips, three for the tongue, one for the teeth. The lips can come together (in various ways); the tongue can lift its tip, its rear, or its rim; the teeth—as you will have guessed— merely bite.

These are the only muscular actions possible, in the task of articulation: yet there are twenty-one consonants in the Alphabet—not counting those consonant-sounds that are made by two letters combined—which means that these few actions have to be varied in many, very delicate ways inside a very small space, and—when strung together into words and sentences—in an incredibly brief space of time. The lips might be likened to castinets, or cymbals—two identical

Release Your Voice and Find Your Personality

percussors acting together; and the tongue-movements to those of triangles and drums—one "agent" being small, thin and active, the other much larger and completely passive.

Make the five basic movements in turn, and see how many speech-sounds you can find for each. As a guide, the first movement—the meeting of the lips—produces the first consonant, B; the lifting of the tongue tip, D; of the tongue back, K. The rim-of-tongue sounds are not so easy to identify, the simplest being Y. (Remember we are dealing with the *sound* of the consonants, not their *name*—if the sounds made by Y and B were "Wy" and "Bee", *young boy* would be pronounced *wyung bee-oy*.) The teeth bite either the tongue—making TH, or the lower lip—making F or V.

Do you bite your lip for the last two sounds, or do you just blow vaguely between nearly-closed lips? And did you realize that TH has two different "noises"—a buzz as in *Though*, or a puff as in *Through*?

This brings us to another speech-fact—one that may come as a surprise. Some of the sounds we make require no voice at all: if we hadn't a larynx we could still articulate them perfectly. Returning to the first consonant B. Make it firmly, then repeat it *without using any vocal sound*. What is left? Something very like P. Repeat it with a little more breath—to compensate for the absence of voice—and the "P" is complete. There are six other pairs like this in the Alphabet—can you identify them? I call them "twin" sounds because they are physically identical.

Now for a glance at some Tongue Tip sounds. What *exactly* does the tip do for each? For D it taps, for J there is a buzz after the tap, for L it flicks, for N it presses. Repeat these four movements quickly several times.... The differences are so slight—involving only a fraction of an inch—that it is easy to see why really polished diction is rare.

Now take the first and last of these four tip sounds—D and N, and make them silently in front of a mirror ... ("D-N—" not Dee—Enn). We know they are different, yet the movements *look* identical. Put back their sound and listen ... with D the sound cannot come until the Tongue drops, and it ends

Our Percussion Instrument

in a flash, as soon as it is made; with N the sound comes *before* the drop and can last as long as you like to keep the tongue up there—or until your breath gives out.

Every Consonant—whether made by tongue, lips or teeth—can be differentiated in this way—as are the Percussion Instruments of the orchestra—some make short sharp sounds, such as castinets and triangles and drums, others can sustain their tones—like the tambourine, which is both tapped and shaken; and the cymbals, which are sometimes damped instantly, sometimes swung and held aloft—with a flourish—so as to prolong the vibrations.

The lip-percussors are deceptive. Often we think we are sounding them when actually we are only *moving* them. P and F particularly—having no vocal tone—are frequently seen-but-not-heard. . . .

The study of articulation is absorbing, and for those who are interested there are numerous textbooks dealing with the subject in full. A brief summary of the facts already touched on is appended to this chapter, in case you care to experiment with them.

Let me add, that a grasp of all these details is not inseparable from clear speaking—if it were, most of us would be reduced to conversing in dumb-show! The make-up of a single consonant is intricate enough, let alone that of a whole word; and if we tried consciously to be aware of each one of the lightning clicks and hums and hisses that take place in every sentence we utter we should end up like the centipede that

> . . . was happy quite
> Until a Toad in fun,
> Inquired—"which leg goes after which?"
> This worked his mind to such a pitch—
> He lay distracted in a ditch,
> Considering how to run!

But merely to know that all these vocal activities exist should help to smarten up your speech. The sub-conscious mind will begin to work for you. It cannot, of course, complete the job without any exertion on your part. Theory must

Release Your Voice and Find Your Personality

be backed up by experiment. . . . In the next chapter you will find some of the commoner faults in diction, with suggestions for overcoming them. The effort is rewarding—not least for the gratification of knowing that you are master of the sounds you make, instead of their being master of you.

Our Percussion Instrument

THE PERCUSSIONS

The character of a "percussor" is built up of its *movement* (as made by lips, tongue or teeth) its *sound* (voiced or breathed) and its *impact* (sharp or smooth).

Here are the MOVEMENTS:
- *Lips*   Bounce—B, P. Press—M. Pout—W.
- *Teeth*   Bite lip—F, V. Bite tongue—TH.
- *Tongue-lifts* Tip—D, L, N, R, T.
  - Rear—G, K, -ng.
  - Rim—Y.
  - Rim and Tip—J, S, Z.
  - Rear to Tip—X.

(You could test your muscular grip of these by finding alliterations to repeat three times quickly—Busy Body, Dare-Devil Dick, Five Fine Fresh Fish, and so on.)

The SOUNDS are:
- "TWINS" (voiced)   B—P (breathed)
  - D—T
  - G—K
  - J—Ch
  - V—F
  - Z—S
- "SINGLE"—Voiced—L, N, R, W
  - —Breathed—H
- "DOUBLE" (i.e. Voiced *or* Breathed)
  - TH, X

(If you sound the first of each "twin", then repeat it with no voice but more breath, you will find you are sounding the second one.

The IMPACTS:
- Sharp —B, D, G, K, P, T
- Smooth—all the others ....

(list them on the dotted line, "testing" each as you write).

Two signs are omitted from these lists—C and Q. C is covered by S and K, and Q is a hybrid, being inseparable—for some reason—from the vowel U (together sounded *koo*).

12

Our Native Tongue

THERE is a real sense of personal satisfaction to be found in polished speaking—an almost sensual pleasure in being able to get the tongue firmly around every word we utter. The lips and teeth as well, of course. But the tongue is by far the busiest sound-maker, and the hardest to manage—as we began to discover, chapters ago, when we tried to get it out of the way of the tone—its position inside the mouth affects the quality of every vowel, and it is directly responsible for quite two-thirds of the consonants.

No wonder languages are known as tongues. . . .

Having learnt to control its stillness, we now have to control its action. To quote St. James, "The Tongue is a little member and boasteth great things." It also doeth quaint things, as I have discovered on seeking to examine the tongues of "woolly" speakers. Sometimes it is thrust out at me in a thick fleshy lump, sometimes it emerges all-of-a-tremble, or in stiff jerks, or switching from side to side, or flopping towards the chin—too flabby to support itself—it will even poke out obliquely, as if to lick the owner's ear.

Does your tongue play tricks like this? If so, it needs some definite drill.

Extend it slowly, as far as it will go—absolutely straight, as though pushing something away with the tip.

Draw a straight line with the extended tip—slowly and smoothly—from one corner of the mouth to the other.

Draw shapes in the air with it—squares, and circles, crosses and triangles.

Tap the chin three times. Tap the nose three times—or as near as you can reach—it's the *stretching* that matters.

Finally, something you need not wait to do in private—

Our Native Tongue

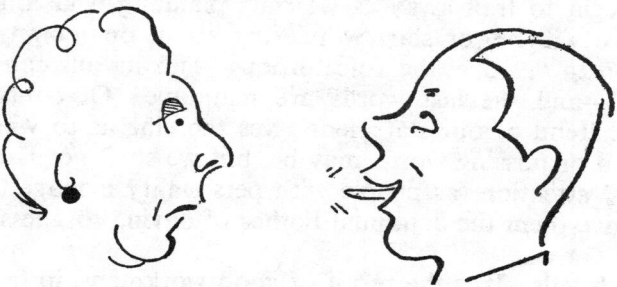

Extend it . . . as far as it will go.

count your teeth with the tip, upper and lower ones alternately, contacting only one tooth at a time.

After this, you should be ready to tackle, fearlessly, the longest place-name in the Welsh Directory.

Our tongue may seem quite strong and supple when tackling the various percussion-sounds singly. How does it behave when these sounds come in rapid succession and all mixed together, as they do in everyday speech? How does it behave in particular—at the *ends* of your words? If I were asked for one broad rule for clear speech I would say—concentrate on word ends. Take care of the finals and the initials will take care of themselves. This is literally true: *finish a word crisply, and you clear the way for the start of the next.*

It is the endings that give the final polish to our delivery, the ends of words, and the ends of sentences. Send your thought forward to the last sound, and your voice will follow.

Most of us *begin* a word clearly enough—as far as the stressed syllable; then our minds run on to the next word, and the next (few people know how a sentence is going to end when they start it)—leaving the tail-pieces to look after themselves, which they naturally fail to do without the conscious brain behind them. Consequently the final syllables become telescoped, and the last letter is inaudible. Words like *impossible* and *continent* become *impossboo* and *cont'n'n*.

The same thing happens with sentences. The first few words are clear—as far as the emphatic word of the group—and then

Release Your Voice and Find Your Personality

they begin to trail away as we start planning what the next sentence will be, or start wondering about our companions reaction to *this* one, the voice droops—lacking our conscious control—and the last words are inaudible. Of course the general trend of our statement gives the clue as to what the drooped or missing words may be, but we shall not *rivet* our hearers' attention (as people with personality manage to do) if we give them the continual bother of having to guess what we say.

Finish tells. It is the proof of good workmanship in every sphere of life. We speak of a well-finished garment, of well-finished furniture; a well-written play has a strong "curtain" to close every scene—and a well-spoken person puts a strong ending to every word he utters.

This may seem a tall order—even a pedantic one—*over* clarity can be maddening, it merely has the effect of making people want *not* to listen. Disproportion is as undesirable in speech as it is in any other form—a body that is "all bone" is no more attractive than one that is too well-covered; it would be an ill-balanced orchestra that allowed its drums and brass to drown the theme borne by the strings—but my remark did not apply to every *sound* uttered: "ex-tra-or-din-ah-reh" is no better than "strorny"—both are incorrect and ugly . . .

As a short-cut to clear speech, it is helpful to know that some finals occur very much more frequently than others. The three tongue-tip sounds S, T and D are the most common. If you concentrate on these, your sub-conscious mind will gradually "get the idea", and you'll find other end-sounds smartening-up, too.

S is one of the characteristic sounds of the English tongue. That is, it is heard—unlike French— in nearly all plurals, present tenses and possessives (and is frequently doubled, as in feminines). For this reason anything odd about it—such as a lisp (or a whistle!)—is immediately noticeable, when other slightly imperfect sounds pass muster.

-t and -d share our past tenses between them. We write walk*ed* and lock*ed*, but we say Walk*t* and lock*t*—that is, we think we do, but we very often let the final letter swamp the true *word*-end (-k, in this case) and all that is actually *heard* is "wort" and "lot". We think we are making the k sound, because we can *feel* its movement, but actually the rear of the tongue sinks back silently to make way for the -d, instead of springing back smartly with a separate click of its own.

A similar thing can happen with certain plurals, "Guests" and "Months" sounding like "Guess" and "Munss". The tip rises for the first of the three final consonants, and lazily stays-put ready for the third, ignoring the one in between.

It is all a matter of *rebound*. Whatever the percussor—tongue tip, tongue rear, teeth, lips—it must end each word with a little bounce, as a drumstick rebounds after every impact.

Avoid the other extreme of vocalizing the bounce—giving the effect of an extra syllable tacked-er on-er at the end-er. (One is reminded of the cleric who admonished his flock to "Lift up your hearts and liver!")

Jot down half a dozen words ending in -g and -k, such as beg, flag, brick, ask. Repeat each—first as it stands, then with -ed added—beg, be*gg-ed*, etc.—the tongue doing a clean see-saw movement from rear to tip. For "a*sked*" the tongue does a double see-saw, tip-rear-tip.

Do the same with words ending in -b and -p: absorb, absor*b-ed*; gasp, ga*sp-ed*; bouncing the lips before each tongue-tap.

Then find some -th -st -ct words and repeat with *s* added: faith, faith-s; cost, cos-t-s; fact, fac-t-s; giving each of the final consonant-sounds its own little separate bounce.

So much for final letters.

There are some final *syllables* that give trouble, not in themselves, but because another part of the word suffers for them.

We say "general" correctly (apart from shortening it to gen'ral perhaps) but directly -*ly* is added, it becomes one of the most ill-used words in our language, being changed to *generly, genally, genry* or even *genny*. If we look into this unlucky word we find that the tongue has four different kinds of percussion to make; no wonder it is tempted to shirk some of them.

Sometimes the same sound is repeated in next-door syllables, and the percussor involved—usually the tongue—makes one sound do for two. Words like Lib*r*ary and Feb*r*uary and Cont*r*ary becoming *Libry, Febry, Contry*. Regu*l*arly and Particu*l*arly become *Reguly* (or *Regly*), and *Particly* (or *tickly* or even *ticky*!). Femi*ni*nity usually ends with a screwed-up nose and a stammer....

Sometimes a repeated *Lip*-sound traps us (Pro*ba*bly becoming *Probly* or *Probby*). And sometimes a repeated *Vowel* sound, as when C*o*nside*ra*bly and P*er*son*a*lly become *C'nsiderby* and *Persny*. In both these words the "er" sound (rightly used for all unstressed syllables) should occur three times.

Watch out for all words ending in -ly, -ry, -ty: that little extra syllable is your danger signal; it seems to make the rest of the word just too much for our *articulative agility*. Now say those last two words three times quickly.

You have already been warned about *overdoing* finals—"quickly" isn't "quickly-er", "quicklee", "quicklay" or even "quickleh", but *quick*lĭ.

There are two other tongue-endings that need care, -ING and -TL (or -DL). In the first, avoid using the wrong end of the tongue.

Jot down some "ing" words:
Bring, Fling, Ring, Sing, Wing.
You would not dream of pronouncing these, Brin', Flin', and so on—which proves that the tongue is perfectly capable of the movement required. Say each word slowly, registering the feel of the last sound, then add another *-ing* to it, thus using exactly the same tongue-action twice over: Bri*ng*, Bri*ng*-i*ng*; Fli*ng*, Fli*ng*-i*ng* and so on. If you anchor the tip behind the lower teeth and drop the jaw well each time, the back of the tongue will find it easier to do the task it had been relegating to the tip.

Sometimes the back of the tongue overdoes it, and gives -ING a click instead of a hum, notably in Birminggam!

Our Native Tongue

TL suffers various translations: "little bottle" can be rendered:

> lit-*t*le bot-*t*le
> likkle bokkle
> lĭ'-l' bŏ'-l'
> li-ŏo bo-ŏo

The first being a case of over-articulation, the second of substitution, and the last two of elimination!

The first is the most frequent, and the most difficult to cure. It separates T and L instead of blending them. The tongue tip should rise to the gum ridge for the T and cling there, not rebounding till *after* the L (one of the few occasions when the tongue is allowed to be lazy!)

Final L's sometimes give trouble on their own account, especially in Kent, where a field can become a "feud" and "label" can sound like *laboo*. But if, in the latter, we lift our tongue tip for the first L, we can equally well lift it for the second—instead of retracting it. . . .

List some final -L words, and give them three extra tongue flicks:

> Fill-li-li-lil, Well-le-le-lel, Ball-la-la-lal,

and so on.

ENDINGS are not the only "catches" of course. We all have our own weak-spots, and I cannot do more than generalize.

Often we mis-speak a word because we don't *look at it* properly. M and N are frequently confused, not because they are awkward to say (except for certain coloured people, who seem to have trouble with "humming" their N's) but because they sound and look alike, and we fail to make note of their relative position in a word. Here are some familiar mixtures:

> Anemone, Anonymous, Diminutive, Enmity, Magnanimity, Unanimity, Phenomenon.

When you find yourself slurring or telescoping a word, don't just say it again louder—blindly (or deafly, rather) hoping for the best. . . . Listen to it, look at it, and *find out why*. There is always a reason, and that reason will help to clean up other words of a similar type. Count the syllables,

Release Your Voice and Find Your Personality

and *sound each one*—however slightly. Every word has one main syllable, the rest are quick and light. The question as to which *is* the main one leads us, again, into the vast realm of Pronunciation (as distinct from Articulation), which does not directly concern a book on Voice.

I use the word "question" because there is still a great deal of controversy on the subject—and quite a bit of snobbery. Should we say *con*troversy or con*trov*ersy? Is it a question of *fi*nance or fi*nance*? A good dictionary will put you right in most cases. Where alternatives are given, keep your ears open for what is "accepted" at the present time. There are fashions in language, as in dress and interior decoration.

You can learn an immense amount from the radio (though I have heard Announcers say pro*blem* and orch*ee*stra and p*er*tic*er*lerly, and an Archbishop say orf*t*en). Keep a pencil handy when you listen or look-in, to make notes of the bad and the good and the unfamiliar.

In your reading, don't allow your eye to skim across "uncertain" words—stop and examine them: and when a word appeals to you *make it yours* by *using* it in conversation at the first opportunity. But don't go *on* using it at *every* opportunity! Word-habits can be as tiresome, to others, as any other kind of personal mannerism. Besides, a word over-used soon becomes meaningless.

This word-collecting helps to give another kind of polish to your speech—adding to good sounds the attraction of good sense. You will find yourself using with confidence words that you have shirked before, through uncertainty. This uncertainty is bound to have its psychological effect: continually to hesitate over a word, and fumble for another—ending up with a feeble substitute, or one that is definitely out of place—does not help to build up one's self-esteem and to mispronounce a word can let one down even more in the esteem of others.

Decisive speech is a wonderful confidence builder. To be sure of your voice, and of your words, will help you to be sure of your *self*, and will certainly lead other people to be sure of you.

Interlude
Getting Down To It

PEOPLE anxious to improve their Speech are fond of asking "how long will it take?"

This depends on many things, not least on their patience. Habits of half a life time cannot be broken—and new ones established—in a week. It also depends on their ear—its sensitivity to the difference between the sounds they are making and the sounds they *should* make. Most of all, as I said at the beginning, it depends on their courage—their willingness to be "different"—especially among friends! *They* know us by our old voice, and it is so easy to go on doing and being what people expect. Strange how we shrink from improving ourselves because of "what people will *say*" . . . Some hesitate to develop a "different" voice for fear of sounding artificial. But it only *seems* so because it *is* different. The old way of speaking was the artificial way, the new way is right and normal.

Their reluctance is understandable. The average Englishman loathes drawing attention to himself, and any virtue carried to extremes can be objectionable. No one wants a resonant voice that is overbearing, "shapely" speech that amounts to "mouthing", clear tones that are intrusive and "edgy" (and produce edginess in others) or vitality that exhausts the listener. But you are unlikely to reach these extremes—your anxiety not to is sufficient proof that you won't. The *really* exaggerated speaker is always blissfully unaware of being tiresome.

The best way to take the plunge is to *start on strangers*—people who can't compare what you are with what you were. Make use of bus-conductors and waitresses; of people who ask you the time, or the way (and if a word or a sentence lets

Release Your Voice and Find Your Personality

you down, make a mental note to be on the alert for it, next time).

You could make a definite start by using your "released voice" the next time you enter a post-office. Formulate in advance the *exact* sentence you are going to use, and make your request "A five-shilling book of stamps, please"—or whatever it may be—with absolute clarity and absolute *confidence*. The man behind the grid won't bat an eyelid (though he'll probably serve you quicker) and you will have cleared your first hurdle. It will be easier, next time.

Decide *always* to take your released voice with you when —say—travelling, or shopping; people are far too preoccupied with their own affairs to notice your speech, unless to admire or even envy—it, and to treat you with extra courtesy, for everyone reacts pleasantly to a pleasant voice. Have you ever noticed a bored shop assistant turn reluctantly to a customer and seen her immediate change of manner when beautifully measured tones address her? The next time you wait your turn at a theatre box-office watch how the man with the pencil alters his demeanour—without raising his eyes—according to the voice that comes to him through his little window.

A shy young nurse told me she first tried her "real voice" on a station platform with triumphant results. She had to change trains with very little time to spare—and wanted to verify her connection. A group of porters stood in deep consultation, their backs towards her. She approached with a firm tread and a deep breath . . . they literally leapt apart and all began directing her in chorus. She declared she's been a new woman ever since.

Soon you will have the courage to pass from strangers to acquaintances. Take advantage of formal occasions, when formal speech is expected of you, and you are less likely to feel awkward about it. Greetings and leave-takings are useful, because they are both formal and frequent and comments on the weather (if you *must* make them). Any of those ready-made phrases that emerge automatically and so leave your mind free to attend to the way they are said. Gradually you

Getting Down to It

will find your Better Speech seeping into the sentence before and the sentence after, till eventually you are using it all the time.

A good plan is to catalogue the sentences you are continually using in your daily occupation.

For instance, a dentist's list would doubtless include "Now show me which one it is" and "Just have a rinse with this". A salesman's—"Can I help you, Madam?" and "Pay at the desk, please". An estate-agent used to practise on me with "Here we have a very attractive property." A homewife (I refuse to use that unattractive label "housewife") compiled the following:

1. How nice to see you!—come in and sit down for a minute.
2. Two pounds of cooking apples, please.
3. Come along, everyone—tea's ready.
4. Don't bang the door, and, wipe your feet.

I am also indebted to a schoolmistress for the following:

Common Sayings of a Common Teacher

1. Quiet now, Children.
2. Sit up, don't polish the desk with your elbows.
3. Go and wash those hands at once, then write that again using half as much ink.
4. Have you a handkerchief? Then use it.
5. Fetch my tea from the staff-room, please, and keep your thumb out of the cup.

Don't expect your speech to be full-toned and well-shaped *and* clear *and* vital all at once: take each required quality in turn. Decide that Monday—say—shall be your resonant day, or that, whatever may happen during the course of a certain morning, you *will* . . . speak . . . slowly . . .

Finally, have a session with a tape recorder. It is a vocal camera that cannot lie. It will reveal truths about your

Release Your Voice and Find Your Personality

speech that you probably would not accept from any human critic, but it will also reassure you as to the *naturalness* of good speech. Sentences that felt laborious or pernickity in the saying will come back to you as perfectly normal—even though you do not recognize the voice that utters them.

13

Cures for Monotony

SOME voices, like some faces, are delightful for ten minutes, but pall on longer acquaintance. It is the same in other spheres. Passing an art shop we are struck by a colourful painting, but the next time we go by its attraction has somehow faded. Our ears catch a lilting tune—we get it on the brain—and a week later wish we could forget it.

What is it that endows a picture or a melody with enduring beauty? We must ask that of the experts. In a face, surely it is character; in a voice, character too—expressed by *change*. Our thoughts are changing every minute; our words are changing every minute; obviously then, the medium we use for expressing these should change every minute in sympathy.

One would imagine the voice couldn't help changing, with so much to encourage it! Yet strange to say, one of the most common faults in everyday speech is monotony. Voices that keep to one "dead" level. Voices that rise and fall, but always in the same way; voices that change their tune, but string their words together like beads—all very small and close together, or very large and heavy, and all exactly the same distance apart; voices that vary their speed and volume but are always bright, or always forlorn *whatever* they are talking about—a party, or a car accident, or a secret, or an insult.... We do our utmost to listen, but gradually our concentration flags and we escape into our own thoughts, "mm-ing" and "oh-ing" at intervals, and trusting that our intonations are appropriate...."

Monotony is generally taken to mean sameness of pitch, but it can apply to any kind of sameness: any particular property in the voice that, though harmless in itself, bores—even irritates—through over-use.

Release Your Voice and Find Your Personality

Let us look at some of these vocal properties, and see how we can control them to the benefit—instead of to the detriment—of our speech.

The subject of pitch has already been discussed in the Loud Speaker chapter, but its possibilities are endless. By varying the pitches of the voice during the course of a sentence—that is, by consciously directing its tune—we can play all sorts of tricks with the meaning. It can have almost as many different implications as it has words.

Take the simple question:
"DID YOU ENJOY THE CONCERT AT THE ALBERT HALL LAST NIGHT?"

Its most obvious tune would start fairly high, dip towards the word "hall" and rise again for the last two words, thus:

DID ⸺⸺⸺⸺ HALL ╱NIGHT?

But by changing the position of the "dip" it is possible to imply:

DID ⸺⸺ NIGHT?   (You surprise me)

DID ╲ YOU ╱ NIGHT?   (Some did, some didn't)

DID ╲ ENJOY ╱ NIGHT?   (I heard it was terrible)

Try changing the tune so as to imply (simply by shifting the "dip" along):

(You generally choose Ballet)
(I thought you went the night before)
(You said you were going to a matinee)

Thus, it is possible to make a *graph* of the human voice. How many graphs—that is, how many meanings (and feelings) can you find for: "HAVE YOU SEEN HER HAT?"

Listen to the tunes in people's speech, and see if you can reproduce them, mentally. On a journey, in a queue—have a pencil handy, and trace the shape of overheard remarks on your shopping-list, or in the margin of your newspaper.

Cures for Monotony

Most important of all, listen to the tunes in your own speech, and if they all sound like a straight line you will know that something is wrong: either your voice is failing fully to express your thought, or you have not yet learnt how to listen. The art of speaking, as I have suggested before, is fifty per cent the art of listening—in the same way that the art of drawing and painting, an artist will tell us, is fifty per cent the art of *seeing*: you cannot be master of that of which you are unaware. . . .

For odd-moment practice, make remarks to yourself such as "What a grand idea", or "That person puzzles me", and trace their shape in the air with one finger; or pick out a short, emphatic sentence from whatever you happen to be reading, say it slowly, with maximum meaning, and then try to reproduce its tune on a humming sound.

So expressive is the human instrument that it dispenses with words entirely, on occasion. Replying to the question "Did you enjoy the Concert at the Albert Hall last night?" a brief "mm" can supply a whole range of comments:

Very much.	Fairly well.
Not particularly	What can one expect?
Definitely not!	Surprisingly, no.
Of course.	What do *you* think?

Repeat these, first as they stand then replaced by a hum or a grunt, whichever is the more appropriate. . . .

Hums and grunts were once our sole means of expression, till primitive man felt the growing urge to communicate, and so he put more and more *change* into his vocal "noises" in order to increase their scope: different types of noise were associated with different thoughts and objects in different parts of the inhabited world—according to the temperaments and habits of their peoples—and so, gradually, languages were born.

But it would seem that, with the development of language —the multiplying of words, the growing complexity of their meanings and the diversity of their grouping—the actual *sound* of it has deteriorated. As the choice of expressive words increased so the need for expressive tones diminished;

Release Your Voice and Find Your Personality

and where once the tune and the loudness and the speed of our "noises" were all-important to the sense, we can now make ourselves understood in a flat drone, provided the words are adequate.

Our words, too, are becoming less adequate, since the advance(?) of mechanized entertainment. Once upon a time people regularly met together for the pleasure of talking; now-a-days millions of us queue—or turn a nob—and sit in the dark, silently gaping at the rehearsed talk of a limited few.

But the theme of Words—their choice and use—could fill another volume, and expressive speech depends less upon the kind of words we use than upon the way we say them—the warmth and vitality we give to this lovely living language of ours.

Probably one of the first words to emerge from our Anglo-Saxon hums and grunts was "oh". This one little syllable, used expressively, can take the place of an entire sentence—of a dozen different sentences, in fact, including:

Is that so?	You don't mean it?
Indeed!	I . . . SEE. . . .!
What a pity.	You *did* give me a start.
How strange . . .	That hurts!
It's scandalous!	Help!!

Can you analyse *exactly* how your voice achieves these remarkable differences in meaning? Decide which vocal "properties" are used for each one—whether you change the tune or the volume or the speed, or all three.

Speed is a "property" of the voice that many of us completely overlook, probably because the rate at which we do things is very much a part of our individual nature.

We each have a deeply ingrained "habit rate" of thinking, moving, eating, writing, reading, talking—bound up, no doubt, with our nervous reactions, our mental outlook, our way of life and many other factors better explained by psychologists than by me. This "personal pace" of ours is not always consistent. We may gobble our food but walk sedately; gabble our words, but be the last to see a joke; write laborious letters, but get through a book in one evening; and these habits

Cures for Monotony

of pace—like all other habits—are none too easy to alter. We should *be able* to alter them, or we are not masters in our own house; we should *practise* altering them, as a little exercise in personal adaptability—a most valuable asset in life—and in thus making ourselves pace-conscious we shall find it easier to vary the pace of our speech.

If you are aware of over-deliberate speaking, consciously speed-up some other activity—make yourself scribble, or—if you already do that—take the stairs two-at-a-time (whenever dignity is not demanded). If—as is more likely—your words rush and tumble (and if especially, you have a tendency to stammer) chew every mouthful of food, and don't allow yourself to skim the news. . . . These deliberate disciplines—in company with the various others scattered through this book —all help to render the mind more flexible, and *we need a flexible mind to achieve a flexible voice.*

To return, for a moment, to the effects achieved by that simple little word OH. In changing your vocal expression you probably changed your facial expression as well. . . . Why not? The face plays a most important part in speech. Its structure— as we have already discovered—affects the quality of the tone; its mobility (or lack of it) affects the light and shade.

Test this. Say "good morning" aloud to yourself, first with bright eyes and smiling mouth; then with a frown; then with a blank look. . . .

Too many voices emerge from deadpan faces, and being dull to watch makes us dull to listen to, even though our tones are varied. Monotony can be visual as well as vocal! People look at our face while we talk, and if it lacks expression it certainly won't help the expressiveness of our words. Relax those facial muscles—allow your mouth and your eyes—yes, even your nose—to do their stuff. . . .

But the face must not be allowed to express *instead* of the voice. It is possible to say a happy sentence with a happy look, and still to use drab tones; just as it is possible to say wounding things with a smile . . . Voice and face and thought should make one harmony.

And here may I add a word about the eyes. Not only *how* we

Release Your Voice and Find Your Personality

look but *where* we look affects our speech—or rather, affects other people's reaction to it—which is just as important. There are two kinds of "lookers" who bore and embarrass. Those who hold our gaze fixedly all the time they are talking, their eyes never leaving ours, and those whose eyes never *meet* ours—who talk doggedly to our shoulder or our ear.

These are quite unconscious habits, no doubt, but they produce a most trying form of monotony.

There is one other sameness that we must strive to avoid, if others are not to avoid *us*. A voice may have every possible change in it, every nuance, every sound-effect, save one. Pause. It just streams on and on . . . This may be a sign of nervousness, certainly it is a sign of lack of poise and control. Nervousness is a form of fear, and some people seem to fear silence, they must fill it with something, however unnecessary and futile. Fear of silence is actually a fear of self, for it is in quietness and stillness that we come face to face with our own personality.

So let me say once again—this time with a different implication—that the art of speaking is very much bound up with the art of listening. Be still, and learn from others—the words they use, the themes they choose. Listen, remember, add to your own mental storehouse. You *know* what *you* would say: there is much more interest and surprise in the conversation of others. And if you are one of those who find it an effort to "join in"—who are not prone to small talk—don't be ashamed or embarrassed by your own silence. There is courage in quietude.

Chapters could be written on the art of vocal change—if the study attracts you, look up "Modulation" in any text-book on Elocution—here I have only space to treat it in the broadest terms; but remember, variety is the spice of speech, and no amount of technique—breath-control and resonance, and good diction—can take its place. Indeed, a rich, clear, controlled voice often *is* monotonous because its owner has got no further than the perfecting of its mechanics. He is like a sculptor who has carved a beautiful statue, but—unlike Pygmalion—has failed to bring it to life.

Cures for Monotony

YET *LIFE* IS THE ONE VITAL ELEMENT BY WHICH THE HUMAN VOICE TRANSCENDS ALL OTHER MEDIUMS OF EXPRESSION. NO OTHER MUSICAL INSTRUMENT CAN CLAIM THIS MAGIC ATTRIBUTE, NO OTHER ART IS LINKED SO CLOSELY AND COMPLETELY WITH THE HUMAN MIND SEEKING TO REVEAL ITSELF. *SPEECH IS A LIVING THING.* ITS SOUNDS ARE MADE BY THE BREATH OF LIFE FLOWING THROUGH LIVING TISSUE; ITS TONES RING WITHIN LIVING BONE, AND ARE SHAPED AND WROUGHT BY LIVING MUSCLE INTO LIVING HUMAN WORDS.

14

Living Words

WE speak a language that is literally "living" for the words we use are, in themselves, alive.

Have you ever realized the extent to which words can be their own interpreters—how their meaning is revealed by the very way in which they are built?

Vivid little words, that we all use, such as:

drip snap trickle ooze screech

There couldn't be any possible doubt as to what these represent.

There are words made up of quick, short syllables to imply quick, short movements, like—*palpitate, fillip* and *ping-pong* (the last a clever invention exactly suggestive of the bounce of that little celluloid ball). Some words are full of s..m..oo..th, s..l..o..w sounds. There are words cold as *ice* and crisp as *toast*; absurd words, like *mulligatawny*; soft ones like *whisper* and *velvet*; hard ones like *castigate* and *granite*.

The significance of words was instilled into me at an early age. My father hated to hear them used carelessly or inexactly, and slang was taboo. If any of the family described something as "rotten" or "foul" he would demand "Has it fallen to pieces yet?" or "What has it to do with farmyards?" Or he would reprove us with remarks such as "beastly is a beastly word". As a consequence, we children used to march around the garden—well out of earshot—chanting: "*Mould*-y is a *mould*-y word!" "*Stink*-ing is a *stink*-ing word!" "*Lous*-y is a *lous*-y word!" taking turns to find the most viscious adjectives. Hardly the result intended. . . . But we certainly became word conscious, and whenever, in reading, I came across a vivid phrase, I used to find myself thinking "Yes,

Living Words

'malignant' *is* a malignant word" or "'Lurid' is a *lurid* word"—and soon I was trying to analyse exactly why . . .

Two words especially took my fancy—*bang* and *strength*. In *bang* the initial letter seemed to me like the initial explosion, the hard short vowel like the ugly sound directly following, and the final hum of -ng like the dwindling echo. *Strength*—with its one short vowel surrounded by seven consonants—symbolized the minimum of flesh held together by the maximum of muscle.

It is a fascinating pastime, examining the structure of words in relation to their sense—the various traits, as it were, that go to make up their personality—especially if we know something of the anatomy of sound as outlined in recent chapters; it would seem that, by bringing out the natural qualities of each—prolonging the sounds that can be prolonged, clipping those that cannot, giving adequate tone to the "voiced" ones, and firm breath to the "breathed"—we shall be making the most of everything we say, and our speech will be not only clear and correct, but *alive* with meaning.

But shall we? And will it? Do these "natural qualities" *always* reflect the sense? Sometimes they help, sometimes they hinder, often a word is so constructed as almost to contradict itself. We find words that need to be light, burdened with heavy sounds, and others needing breadth, bristling with quick ones—for words, like people, have certain attributes that can, if *allowed* spoil their whole nature.

Let us glance at half a dozen:

villain fool short table boy mother

Villain and *fool*, with their soft initials and smooth l's (and that cooing *oo*) are far too mild, as they stand, so to speak; both words need vocal attack to give the right effect. *Short* (like its near relative *sharp*) has only one helpful sound, the last. The *sh* and the long vowel are both smooth by nature, and have to be *made* "short" (and "sharp")!

Table and *boy* are completely negative. They might as well be *chair* and *girl*, or *cup* and *hat*! We must either add an adjective, or *imply an adjective with our voice*—conveying by its tones whether the table is massive or dainty, and the boy

Release Your Voice and Find Your Personality

naughty or comic or pathetic—or any other of the 101 things a boy can be.

Some words in fact, mean nothing, in themselves; their life —or death—depends entirely on what we—literally—*breathe* into them....

You may think these remarks are completely obvious. That "sound effects" come instinctively, if one's mind is on what one is saying. But I have heard so much daily conversation that witnesses to the contrary—streams of devitalized words entirely divorced from the ideas they are intended to express. And the pity is, that many who talk thus are doing *themselves*—as well as their voice—an injustice—making utterly dreary that which, with a little knowledge and vision, could charm everyone's ear.

Sir Winston Churchill is complete master of the words he uses. His utterance of an adjective like "rascally", for instance, is a dragging rasp that perfectly personifies the word, and his classic treatment of the name "Nazi"—with its nasal "ah" and slimy "z"—conjures a mental picture of slugs rather than men: it once caught the imagination of a nation, and fear was changed to contempt. That one word, spoken by a genius, was probably our first step to victory.

The dull muddiness of the word *mother* was brought home to me by a class-student who gave us all a mild shock by saying that he hated the word, and always used "Mater". There was a murmur of dissent from everyone. But, on consideration, we had to admit that the two dull vowels *ŭ* and *er*, either side of the characterless *th* convey nothing, all the onus is on the M—fortunately the most musical of consonants—and the whole word needs to be spoken gently and warmly—as it generally is, by those for whom it has tender associations.

Are there any words that you especially like or dislike? Jot some of them down, and try to discover whether it is the sound of them or the *sense* of them that actually affects you.

It is difficult to disassociate sound from meaning—to dissect words in cold blood, as it were, especially if they are in

Living Words

common use. Only when they are unfamiliar is it possible to treat them dispassionately, and so hear precisely what they sound like.

Some students were discussing this: among them, a Spanish girl who knew very little English. It was suggested that she should listen to their conversation and stop them directly any word particularly caught her fancy. They began—conventionally—with the weather, and this led inevitably to coal. . . . Suddenly she exclaimed "Ah, that is beautiful—'cellar-door'—is it the name of a girl, or a flower?"

Certainly, by the way she said them, the two words had music—but would an English person ever have detected it? Spelt differently, they could make quite an attractive name, and someone took out a pencil and wrote "Selladore". The old sounds with a new look: *their whole character—released from the habits of association—transformed, through a change of thought* . . .

Four of the most significant words in our language—*God, Live, Love, Death*—are most unsuitably devised. *God* with its short vowel squeezed between two sharp consonants (so much less expressive than *Lord* and *Father*); *Live* and *Love* with their tuneless *ĭ* and *ŭ* and vague finish—redeemed by the smooth music of the initial L; and *Death* with its hard start, brief vowel and toneless final—all must rely on the "thought behind the word": that intangeable something which seeps into the voice—if, *backed by knowledge*, it is used imaginatively and sincerely.

The names of flowers vary in appropriateness; in *Daffodil* one can almost see its golden head nodding in the breeze, taking "the winds of March with beauty". *Jonquil* is a pleasing word to look at, but jerky in sound—with little suggestion of daintiness and fragrance—unless five of the seven letters are taken carefully in hand: the *J* and *q* softened, the unpleasing *o* and *i* prolonged, and the *n* and *l* caressed by the voice—whilst the mind visualises the flower's slim beauty . . .

Knowledge of sound-values plus the gift of imagination—these two are inseparable and indispensible if we desire that lovely possession—a musical *and* expressive speaking voice.

15

Voice and Vision

THE whole art of speech—in the final analysis—is the art of transmitting mind-pictures.

An idea comes into our consciousness, and simultaneously—whether we are aware of it or not—comes the mental image of that idea. This image (until such time as we have all acquired the gift of mind-reading) has to be translated into words before it can reach our hearers, who must, in their turn, convert those words into a picture again before its message can "get through".

Obviously, the clearer and better-chosen our words, and the more "alive" our voice (and face), the clearer and more vital will be the message conveyed; and if the picture received differs from the one transmitted, then it is less the fault of our actual words than of our *treatment* of them; for excellent though it is to have a wide vocabulary, the tones and tunes of the voice translate our thought—as I have said before—in a way that words alone can never do.

But those tones and tunes will have little meaning unless there is imagination behind them. A voice may rise and fall, soften or stress, quicken or slacken and pause most impressively —yet only succeed in drawing attention to *itself* instead of to the idea it is supposed to convey. Conversely, if there are *no* vocal changes, the resultant thought-picture will be dull and colourless. But if mind and voice are in complete sympathy then together they will illuminate our words as a shaft of sunlight illumines a picture on a shadowed wall.

Light creates colour. (As the poet puts it—"every cat in the twilight's grey") and it is the light of *imagin*-ation that puts colour into our speech.

Voice and Vision

CONTROLLED BREATH PUTS POWER INTO IT; RESONANCE GIVES IT RICHNESS; SHAPED VOWELS AND MUSCULAR CONSONANTS HELP TO MAKE IT CLEAR AND CONVINCING; VARIETY GIVES IT INTEREST; BUT IT IS THIS MENTAL IMAG-ING—THIS *LIGHT FROM WITHIN* THAT FINALLY ENDOWS IT WITH THE WARMTH AND COLOUR OF THE LIVING PERSONALITY.

If you want to develop colourful tones, practise saying the *names* of colours: vivid in themselves, even before your voice and thought get to work on them.

"Brown" *sounds* brown if you see-it-as-you-say-it: your *voice*—knowing its job—will dwell on the low-pitched opening "burr", and the full round vowel, and the humming -n; and your *thought* will give the word a mellow warmth suggestive of that homely shade.

"Grey" sounds what it is—misty and nebulous—provided you soften its opening growl, and linger on that long pale *a* ...

Your saying of "Blue" can conjure dark depths of ocean, or infinities of bright sky—according to the picture it brings to your mind: but if there is no picture, or if you are unaware of what a smooth *l* and a long *oo* can do for a word and what change of pitch can do for a voice, then "blue" will only sound like a tiny blot of faded ink.

In other words as I have said before knowledge and vision must go together in our quest for colourful speech. The picture alone is powerless. We may muster all our concentration—we may fill our thought with the idea to be "put over" —with no effect whatever on the *voice*, unless it has learnt to obey the mind.

We must have the vocal technique to enable us to reveal the mental picture; but *there must be a picture first*. The most perfect voice control cannot reveal what isn't there.

To return to our colours. "Green"—to me—is cool and clear; "yellow" gay and bright ... but are they? *Only if the mind sees them as such.* The green can be drab, the yellow glaring, *if that is what we wish to convey*. Thus the voice—linked with the imagination—can transmit not merely the colour, but the *shade* of the colour, and our personal *reaction* to that colour—our like or dislike of it.

Release Your Voice and Find Your Personality

A group of stage folk were discussing the emotional attractions—and distractions—of colour. Among them, that fine actress and writer Nancy Price. Suddenly, "I loathe—*pink*!" came that deep, forthright voice of hers, and the glare of that single monosyllable convinced us that no hue could be more hideous!

The voice can do more than comment on a colour, it can actually change it! Say "Black" in a high light tone, and "White" in a low, heavy one, and your voice will turn black into white and white into black. . . .

One begins to catch a glimpse of the power of words in the mouths of great orators. Elizabeth I knew something of that power. The story is told of her making a certain request to two noblemen, one of whom she mistrusted, the other, loved. She addressed the first in cold, hard tones—"Sir X! I entreat you!" then turned gently to the second, and murmured "Sir Y . . . I —command *you* . . ." Her words were chosen for policy, but her voice revealed her heart.

Your voice can reveal your heart—unless you are ashamed of what is hidden there. If you are, read on.

Finale
Your Voice and the Real You

WHEN we find ourselves admiring or disliking a certain type of voice, what we are really doing is admiring or disliking a certain type of person—as reflected in that voice. To us, the voice *is* the person. And if someone whose tones sound like cracking wood proves to be charming, and someone else with mellifluous accents turns out to be a rotter, we know that both voices are being wrongly used: one with the best intentions in the world—but probably with a contracted throat—the other with a fine instrument but with intentions not so fine.

When once the voice is freed, by complete understanding, and used with complete sincerity, the character shines through the speech.

Make a list of the qualities of voice that most appeal to you. Then against each write the personal attributes it suggests. You will probably find you are writing the same word again, or a very similar one. For instance, a deep voice could suggest depth of character; crisp speech could imply crisp thinking; bright tones—a bright outlook; an even voice—an even temper; a gentle voice—gentleness, and so on.

You may disagree! You may contend that a deep voice, if it is woolly, can mean indulgence, or laziness; crisp speech, if it is hard, can mean lack of sympathy; bright tones—superficiality; that evenness of utterance is as likely to indicate a slow mind as a calm one, and gentle speech—mere indecision. Besides, people can camouflage their voices—if they are clever enough—in order to gain their own ends.

All of which is true. One quality may counteract another—in speech, as in personality; different types of voice have different meanings for different people—just as tunes and colours

Release Your Voice and Find Your Personality

have—and anyone can do what he likes with his voice, once he knows how.

That is the crux of the whole matter—*you can do what you like with your own voice.* You can release its power, enrich its tone, polish up its sounds, and vary its tunes at will. You can make it express just what you want it to express. You can develop in it all the qualities that you most admire, and you can avoid anything about it that seems to you undesirable, and *which is actually out of harmony with the real YOU.*

Suppose, for instance, you are aware of a certain harshness in your voice. You should, with practise—now that you know the rules—be able to develop warmer, more sympathetic tones; and in doing so you will find you are opening up the way to acquiring a warmer, more sympathetic character—although possibly you were unaware of that inner need, till now.

You may consider the process should be reversed. That one must first put the heart right, and the voice will follow.

But *that is just what you will be doing.* The fact that you earnestly desire a certain quality in your voice means, in reality, that you desire that quality in *yourself.* And the very fact that you do desire it is proof that this particular quality is already there, latent within you, waiting to be released with your true voice.

What has held it back? For your Voice *is* you; and if it isn't expressing you there is a definite reason. Either it doesn't know how to (and that is already remedied, if you have read thus far) or else it doesn't wish to—because it dislikes what it would be called upon to express. . . . In other words, because you have something to hide. Which brings us to the most important point of all—the climax of our voice studies.

You belong to *You.* All that you feel and think and say and do is yours to decide and direct. If you want to be different you *can* be different. For no desire comes to us without the ability to fulfil it. You are in your own hands, and assuredly you are in your own voice.

If you are aware of certain personal traits that, secretly, you deplore, I am convinced that to take your voice deliberately in hand, and to *will* into it those qualities of tone and speech that suggest the kind of personality you truly wish for, is to take a quite definite step towards acquiring that personality.

Make another list, this time of the vocal traits you dislike, and write against them the human traits with which you would associate them.

Now take the two lists, and tick off—in absolute honesty—each quality, good or bad, that you consider your own voice possesses (or did possess, before you tried out the experiments in this book!). You will have arrived at a pretty accurate estimate of your own character.

Go through the two lists again, and underline the qualities you are now striving for, and cross out those you are determined to avoid. . . .

Do you see how, in choosing a voice for yourself you are also choosing a personality? You are, in effect, deciding not only what you want to sound like, but what you want to *be*.

You must of course bear in mind the basic characteristics of your particular instrument. If it is fundamentally light (and if you have no call to use it on the public platform) you will concentrate on roundness and sweetness of tone, rather than depth; if it is naturally deep and strong you may try for more flexibility—but in neither case must you strain it away from its natural weight and compass, however much a particular way of speaking may appeal to you in other people.

Your ideal is not so much a *new* voice as a *renewed* voice. A voice and an individuality released from the old chains of habit and doubt. The same You with a fresh outlook, and therefore expressing itself in a fresh way.

MELVIN POWERS SELF-IMPROVEMENT LIBRARY

ASTROLOGY

_____ ASTROLOGY: HOW TO CHART YOUR HOROSCOPE *Max Heindel*	3.00
_____ ASTROLOGY AND SEXUAL ANALYSIS *Morris C. Goodman*	5.00
_____ ASTROLOGY MADE EASY *Astarte*	3.00
_____ ASTROLOGY MADE PRACTICAL *Alexandra Kayhle*	3.00
_____ ASTROLOGY, ROMANCE, YOU AND THE STARS *Anthony Norvell*	4.00
_____ MY WORLD OF ASTROLOGY *Sydney Omarr*	7.00
_____ THOUGHT DIAL *Sydney Omarr*	4.00
_____ WHAT THE STARS REVEAL ABOUT THE MEN IN YOUR LIFE *Thelma White*	3.00

BRIDGE

_____ BRIDGE BIDDING MADE EASY *Edwin B. Kantar*	10.00
_____ BRIDGE CONVENTIONS *Edwin B. Kantar*	7.00
_____ BRIDGE HUMOR *Edwin B. Kantar*	5.00
_____ COMPETITIVE BIDDING IN MODERN BRIDGE *Edgar Kaplan*	4.00
_____ DEFENSIVE BRIDGE PLAY COMPLETE *Edwin B. Kantar*	15.00
_____ GAMESMAN BRIDGE—Play Better with Kantar *Edwin B. Kantar*	5.00
_____ HOW TO IMPROVE YOUR BRIDGE *Alfred Sheinwold*	5.00
_____ IMPROVING YOUR BIDDING SKILLS *Edwin B. Kantar*	4.00
_____ INTRODUCTION TO DECLARER'S PLAY *Edwin B. Kantar*	5.00
_____ INTRODUCTION TO DEFENDER'S PLAY *Edwin B. Kantar*	3.00
_____ KANTAR FOR THE DEFENSE *Edwin B. Kantar*	5.00
_____ KANTAR FOR THE DEFENSE VOLUME 2 *Edwin B. Kantar*	7.00
_____ SHORT CUT TO WINNING BRIDGE *Alfred Sheinwold*	3.00
_____ TEST YOUR BRIDGE PLAY *Edwin B. Kantar*	5.00
_____ VOLUME 2—TEST YOUR BRIDGE PLAY *Edwin B. Kantar*	5.00
_____ WINNING DECLARER PLAY *Dorothy Hayden Truscott*	5.00

BUSINESS, STUDY & REFERENCE

_____ CONVERSATION MADE EASY *Elliot Russell*	4.00
_____ EXAM SECRET *Dennis B. Jackson*	3.00
_____ FIX-IT BOOK *Arthur Symons*	2.00
_____ HOW TO DEVELOP A BETTER SPEAKING VOICE *M. Hellier*	4.00
_____ HOW TO MAKE A FORTUNE IN REAL ESTATE *Albert Winnikoff*	4.00
_____ HOW TO SELF-PUBLISH YOUR BOOK & MAKE IT A BEST SELLER *Melvin Powers*	10.00
_____ INCREASE YOUR LEARNING POWER *Geoffrey A. Dudley*	3.00
_____ PRACTICAL GUIDE TO BETTER CONCENTRATION *Melvin Powers*	3.00
_____ PRACTICAL GUIDE TO PUBLIC SPEAKING *Maurice Forley*	5.00
_____ 7 DAYS TO FASTER READING *William S. Schaill*	3.00
_____ SONGWRITERS' RHYMING DICTIONARY *Jane Shaw Whitfield*	6.00
_____ SPELLING MADE EASY *Lester D. Basch & Dr. Milton Finkelstein*	3.00
_____ STUDENT'S GUIDE TO BETTER GRADES *J. A. Rickard*	3.00
_____ TEST YOURSELF—Find Your Hidden Talent *Jack Shafer*	3.00
_____ YOUR WILL & WHAT TO DO ABOUT IT *Attorney Samuel G. Kling*	4.00

CALLIGRAPHY

_____ ADVANCED CALLIGRAPHY *Katherine Jeffares*	7.00
_____ CALLIGRAPHER'S REFERENCE BOOK *Anne Leptich & Jacque Evans*	7.00
_____ CALLIGRAPHY—The Art of Beautiful Writing *Katherine Jeffares*	7.00
_____ CALLIGRAPHY FOR FUN & PROFIT *Anne Leptich & Jacque Evans*	7.00
_____ CALLIGRAPHY MADE EASY *Tina Serafini*	7.00

CHESS & CHECKERS

_____ BEGINNER'S GUIDE TO WINNING CHESS *Fred Reinfeld*	5.00
_____ CHESS IN TEN EASY LESSONS *Larry Evans*	5.00
_____ CHESS MADE EASY *Milton L. Hanauer*	3.00
_____ CHESS PROBLEMS FOR BEGINNERS *edited by Fred Reinfeld*	2.00
_____ CHESS SECRETS REVEALED *Fred Reinfeld*	2.00
_____ CHESS TACTICS FOR BEGINNERS *edited by Fred Reinfeld*	4.00
_____ CHESS THEORY & PRACTICE *Morry & Mitchell*	2.00
_____ HOW TO WIN AT CHECKERS *Fred Reinfeld*	3.00
_____ 1001 BRILLIANT WAYS TO CHECKMATE *Fred Reinfeld*	4.00
_____ 1001 WINNING CHESS SACRIFICES & COMBINATIONS *Fred Reinfeld*	4.00
_____ SOVIET CHESS *Edited by R. G. Wade*	3.00

COOKERY & HERBS

____	CULPEPER'S HERBAL REMEDIES *Dr. Nicholas Culpeper*	3.00
____	FAST GOURMET COOKBOOK *Poppy Cannon*	2.50
____	GINSENG The Myth & The Truth *Joseph P. Hou*	3.00
____	HEALING POWER OF HERBS *May Bethel*	4.00
____	HEALING POWER OF NATURAL FOODS *May Bethel*	3.00
____	HERB HANDBOOK *Dawn MacLeod*	3.00
____	HERBS FOR COOKING AND HEALING *Dr. Donald Law*	2.00
____	HERBS FOR HEALTH—How to Grow & Use Them *Louise Evans Doole*	4.00
____	HOME GARDEN COOKBOOK—Delicious Natural Food Recipes *Ken Kraft*	3.00
____	MEDICAL HERBALIST *edited by Dr. J. R. Yemm*	3.00
____	NATURE'S MEDICINES *Richard Lucas*	3.00
____	VEGETABLE GARDENING FOR BEGINNERS *Hugh Wiberg*	2.00
____	VEGETABLES FOR TODAY'S GARDENS *R. Milton Carleton*	2.00
____	VEGETARIAN COOKERY *Janet Walker*	4.00
____	VEGETARIAN COOKING MADE EASY & DELECTABLE *Veronica Vezza*	3.00
____	VEGETARIAN DELIGHTS—A Happy Cookbook for Health *K. R. Mehta*	2.00
____	VEGETARIAN GOURMET COOKBOOK *Joyce McKinnel*	3.00

GAMBLING & POKER

____	ADVANCED POKER STRATEGY & WINNING PLAY *A. D. Livingston*	5.00
____	HOW NOT TO LOSE AT POKER *Jeffrey Lloyd Castle*	3.00
____	HOW TO WIN AT DICE GAMES *Skip Frey*	3.00
____	HOW TO WIN AT POKER *Terence Reese & Anthony T. Watkins*	5.00
____	WINNING AT CRAPS *Dr. Lloyd T. Commins*	4.00
____	WINNING AT GIN *Chester Wander & Cy Rice*	3.00
____	WINNING AT POKER—An Expert's Guide *John Archer*	5.00
____	WINNING AT 21—An Expert's Guide *John Archer*	5.00
____	WINNING POKER SYSTEMS *Norman Zadeh*	3.00

HEALTH

____	BEE POLLEN *Lynda Lyngheim & Jack Scagnetti*	3.00
____	DR. LINDNER'S SPECIAL WEIGHT CONTROL METHOD *P. G. Lindner, M.D.*	2.00
____	HELP YOURSELF TO BETTER SIGHT *Margaret Darst Corbett*	3.00
____	HOW TO IMPROVE YOUR VISION *Dr. Robert A. Kraskin*	3.00
____	HOW YOU CAN STOP SMOKING PERMANENTLY *Ernest Caldwell*	3.00
____	MIND OVER PLATTER *Peter G. Lindner, M.D.*	3.00
____	NATURE'S WAY TO NUTRITION & VIBRANT HEALTH *Robert J. Scrutton*	3.00
____	NEW CARBOHYDRATE DIET COUNTER *Patti Lopez-Pereira*	2.00
____	QUICK & EASY EXERCISES FOR FACIAL BEAUTY *Judy Smith-deal*	2.00
____	QUICK & EASY EXERCISES FOR FIGURE BEAUTY *Judy Smith-deal*	2.00
____	REFLEXOLOGY *Dr. Maybelle Segal*	3.00
____	REFLEXOLOGY FOR GOOD HEALTH *Anna Kaye & Don C. Matchan*	4.00
____	30 DAYS TO BEAUTIFUL LEGS *Dr. Marc Selner*	3.00
____	YOU CAN LEARN TO RELAX *Dr. Samuel Gutwirth*	3.00
____	YOUR ALLERGY—What To Do About It *Allan Knight, M.D.*	3.00

HOBBIES

____	BEACHCOMBING FOR BEGINNERS *Norman Hickin*	2.00
____	BLACKSTONE'S MODERN CARD TRICKS *Harry Blackstone*	3.00
____	BLACKSTONE'S SECRETS OF MAGIC *Harry Blackstone*	3.00
____	COIN COLLECTING FOR BEGINNERS *Burton Hobson & Fred Reinfeld*	3.00
____	ENTERTAINING WITH ESP *Tony 'Doc' Shiels*	2.00
____	400 FASCINATING MAGIC TRICKS YOU CAN DO *Howard Thurston*	4.00
____	HOW I TURN JUNK INTO FUN AND PROFIT *Sari*	3.00
____	HOW TO WRITE A HIT SONG & SELL IT *Tommy Boyce*	7.00
____	JUGGLING MADE EASY *Rudolf Dittrich*	3.00
____	MAGIC FOR ALL AGES *Walter Gibson*	4.00
____	MAGIC MADE EASY *Byron Wels*	2.00
____	STAMP COLLECTING FOR BEGINNERS *Burton Hobson*	3.00

HORSE PLAYERS' WINNING GUIDES

____	BETTING HORSES TO WIN *Les Conklin*	3.00
____	ELIMINATE THE LOSERS *Bob McKnight*	3.00
____	HOW TO PICK WINNING HORSES *Bob McKnight*	5.00

____ HOW TO WIN AT THE RACES *Sam (The Genius) Lewin*	5.00
____ HOW YOU CAN BEAT THE RACES *Jack Kavanagh*	5.00
____ MAKING MONEY AT THE RACES *David Barr*	3.00
____ PAYDAY AT THE RACES *Les Conklin*	3.00
____ SMART HANDICAPPING MADE EASY *William Bauman*	5.00
____ SUCCESS AT THE HARNESS RACES *Barry Meadow*	5.00
____ WINNING AT THE HARNESS RACES—An Expert's Guide *Nick Cammarano*	5.00

HUMOR

____ HOW TO BE A COMEDIAN FOR FUN & PROFIT *King & Laufer*	2.00
____ HOW TO FLATTEN YOUR TUSH *Coach Marge Reardon*	2.00
____ HOW TO MAKE LOVE TO YOURSELF *Ron Stevens & Joy Grdnic*	3.00
____ JOKE TELLER'S HANDBOOK *Bob Orben*	4.00
____ JOKES FOR ALL OCCASIONS *Al Schock*	4.00
____ 2000 NEW LAUGHS FOR SPEAKERS *Bob Orben*	5.00
____ 2,500 JOKES TO START 'EM LAUGHING *Bob Orben*	5.00

HYPNOTISM

____ ADVANCED TECHNIQUES OF HYPNOSIS *Melvin Powers*	3.00
____ BRAINWASHING AND THE CULTS *Paul A. Verdier, Ph.D.*	3.00
____ CHILDBIRTH WITH HYPNOSIS *William S. Kroger, M.D.*	5.00
____ HOW TO SOLVE Your Sex Problems with Self-Hypnosis *Frank S. Caprio, M.D.*	5.00
____ HOW TO STOP SMOKING THRU SELF-HYPNOSIS *Leslie M. LeCron*	3.00
____ HOW TO USE AUTO-SUGGESTION EFFECTIVELY *John Duckworth*	3.00
____ HOW YOU CAN BOWL BETTER USING SELF-HYPNOSIS *Jack Heise*	3.00
____ HOW YOU CAN PLAY BETTER GOLF USING SELF-HYPNOSIS *Jack Heise*	3.00
____ HYPNOSIS AND SELF-HYPNOSIS *Bernard Hollander, M.D.*	3.00
____ HYPNOTISM *(Originally published in 1893) Carl Sextus*	5.00
____ HYPNOTISM & PSYCHIC PHENOMENA *Simeon Edmunds*	4.00
____ HYPNOTISM MADE EASY *Dr. Ralph Winn*	5.00
____ HYPNOTISM MADE PRACTICAL *Louis Orton*	5.00
____ HYPNOTISM REVEALED *Melvin Powers*	2.00
____ HYPNOTISM TODAY *Leslie LeCron and Jean Bordeaux, Ph.D.*	5.00
____ MODERN HYPNOSIS *Lesley Kuhn & Salvatore Russo, Ph.D.*	5.00
____ NEW CONCEPTS OF HYPNOSIS *Bernard C. Gindes, M.D.*	5.00
____ NEW SELF-HYPNOSIS *Paul Adams*	5.00
____ POST-HYPNOTIC INSTRUCTIONS—Suggestions for Therapy *Arnold Furst*	5.00
____ PRACTICAL GUIDE TO SELF-HYPNOSIS *Melvin Powers*	3.00
____ PRACTICAL HYPNOTISM *Philip Magonet, M.D.*	3.00
____ SECRETS OF HYPNOTISM *S. J. Van Pelt, M.D.*	5.00
____ SELF-HYPNOSIS A Conditioned-Response Technique *Laurence Sparks*	5.00
____ SELF-HYPNOSIS Its Theory, Technique & Application *Melvin Powers*	3.00
____ THERAPY THROUGH HYPNOSIS *edited by Raphael H. Rhodes*	4.00

JUDAICA

____ MODERN ISRAEL *Lily Edelman*	2.00
____ SERVICE OF THE HEART *Evelyn Garfiel, Ph.D.*	4.00
____ STORY OF ISRAEL IN COINS *Jean & Maurice Gould*	2.00
____ STORY OF ISRAEL IN STAMPS *Maxim & Gabriel Shamir*	1.00
____ TONGUE OF THE PROPHETS *Robert St. John*	5.00

JUST FOR WOMEN

____ COSMOPOLITAN'S GUIDE TO MARVELOUS MEN Fwd. by *Helen Gurley Brown*	3.00
____ COSMOPOLITAN'S HANG-UP HANDBOOK Foreword by *Helen Gurley Brown*	4.00
____ COSMOPOLITAN'S LOVE BOOK—A Guide to Ecstasy in Bed	5.00
____ COSMOPOLITAN'S NEW ETIQUETTE GUIDE Fwd. by *Helen Gurley Brown*	4.00
____ I AM A COMPLEAT WOMAN *Doris Hagopian & Karen O'Connor Sweeney*	3.00
____ JUST FOR WOMEN—A Guide to the Female Body *Richard E. Sand, M.D.*	5.00
____ NEW APPROACHES TO SEX IN MARRIAGE *John E. Eichenlaub, M.D.*	3.00
____ SEXUALLY ADEQUATE FEMALE *Frank S. Caprio, M.D.*	3.00
____ SEXUALLY FULFILLED WOMAN *Dr. Rachel Copelan*	5.00
____ YOUR FIRST YEAR OF MARRIAGE *Dr. Tom McGinnis*	3.00

MARRIAGE, SEX & PARENTHOOD

____ ABILITY TO LOVE *Dr. Allan Fromme*	6.00

___	GUIDE TO SUCCESSFUL MARRIAGE *Drs. Albert Ellis & Robert Harper*	5.00
___	HOW TO RAISE AN EMOTIONALLY HEALTHY, HAPPY CHILD *A. Ellis*	4.00
___	SEX WITHOUT GUILT *Albert Ellis, Ph.D.*	5.00
___	SEXUALLY ADEQUATE MALE *Frank S. Caprio, M.D.*	3.00
___	SEXUALLY FULFILLED MAN *Dr. Rachel Copelan*	5.00

MELVIN POWERS' MAIL ORDER LIBRARY

___	HOW TO GET RICH IN MAIL ORDER *Melvin Powers*	15.00
___	HOW TO WRITE A GOOD ADVERTISEMENT *Victor O. Schwab*	15.00
___	MAIL ORDER MADE EASY *J. Frank Brumbaugh*	10.00
___	U.S. MAIL ORDER SHOPPER'S GUIDE *Susan Spitzer*	10.00

METAPHYSICS & OCCULT

___	BOOK OF TALISMANS, AMULETS & ZODIACAL GEMS *William Pavitt*	5.00
___	CONCENTRATION—A Guide to Mental Mastery *Mouni Sadhu*	5.00
___	CRITIQUES OF GOD *Edited by Peter Angeles*	7.00
___	EXTRA-TERRESTRIAL INTELLIGENCE—The First Encounter	6.00
___	FORTUNE TELLING WITH CARDS *P. Foli*	4.00
___	HANDWRITING ANALYSIS MADE EASY *John Marley*	4.00
___	HANDWRITING TELLS *Nadya Olyanova*	5.00
___	HOW TO INTERPRET DREAMS, OMENS & FORTUNE TELLING SIGNS *Gettings*	3.00
___	HOW TO UNDERSTAND YOUR DREAMS *Geoffrey A. Dudley*	3.00
___	ILLUSTRATED YOGA *William Zorn*	3.00
___	IN DAYS OF GREAT PEACE *Mouni Sadhu*	3.00
___	LSD—THE AGE OF MIND *Bernard Roseman*	2.00
___	MAGICIAN—His Training and Work *W. E. Butler*	3.00
___	MEDITATION *Mouni Sadhu*	7.00
___	MODERN NUMEROLOGY *Morris C. Goodman*	3.00
___	NUMEROLOGY—ITS FACTS AND SECRETS *Ariel Yvon Taylor*	3.00
___	NUMEROLOGY MADE EASY *W. Mykian*	4.00
___	PALMISTRY MADE EASY *Fred Gettings*	5.00
___	PALMISTRY MADE PRACTICAL *Elizabeth Daniels Squire*	4.00
___	PALMISTRY SECRETS REVEALED *Henry Frith*	3.00
___	PROPHECY IN OUR TIME *Martin Ebon*	2.50
___	PSYCHOLOGY OF HANDWRITING *Nadya Olyanova*	5.00
___	SUPERSTITION—Are You Superstitious? *Eric Maple*	2.00
___	TAROT *Mouni Sadhu*	8.00
___	TAROT OF THE BOHEMIANS *Papus*	5.00
___	WAYS TO SELF-REALIZATION *Mouni Sadhu*	3.00
___	WHAT YOUR HANDWRITING REVEALS *Albert E. Hughes*	3.00
___	WITCHCRAFT, MAGIC & OCCULTISM—A Fascinating History *W. B. Crow*	5.00
___	WITCHCRAFT—THE SIXTH SENSE *Justine Glass*	5.00
___	WORLD OF PSYCHIC RESEARCH *Hereward Carrington*	2.00

SELF-HELP & INSPIRATIONAL

___	DAILY POWER FOR JOYFUL LIVING *Dr. Donald Curtis*	5.00
___	DYNAMIC THINKING *Melvin Powers*	2.00
___	GREATEST POWER IN THE UNIVERSE *U. S. Andersen*	5.00
___	GROW RICH WHILE YOU SLEEP *Ben Sweetland*	3.00
___	GROWTH THROUGH REASON *Albert Ellis, Ph.D.*	4.00
___	GUIDE TO PERSONAL HAPPINESS *Albert Ellis, Ph.D. & Irving Becker, Ed. D.*	5.00
___	HELPING YOURSELF WITH APPLIED PSYCHOLOGY *R. Henderson*	2.00
___	HOW TO ATTRACT GOOD LUCK *A. H. Z. Carr*	5.00
___	HOW TO DEVELOP A WINNING PERSONALITY *Martin Panzer*	5.00
___	HOW TO DEVELOP AN EXCEPTIONAL MEMORY *Young & Gibson*	5.00
___	HOW TO LIVE WITH A NEUROTIC *Albert Ellis, Ph. D.*	5.00
___	HOW TO OVERCOME YOUR FEARS *M. P. Leahy, M.D.*	3.00
___	HOW YOU CAN HAVE CONFIDENCE AND POWER *Les Giblin*	5.00
___	HUMAN PROBLEMS & HOW TO SOLVE THEM *Dr. Donald Curtis*	5.00
___	I CAN *Ben Sweetland*	5.00
___	I WILL *Ben Sweetland*	3.00
___	LEFT-HANDED PEOPLE *Michael Barsley*	5.00
___	MAGIC IN YOUR MIND *U. S. Andersen*	6.00
___	MAGIC OF THINKING BIG *Dr. David J. Schwartz*	3.00

___	MAGIC POWER OF YOUR MIND *Walter M. Germain*	5.00
___	MENTAL POWER THROUGH SLEEP SUGGESTION *Melvin Powers*	3.00
___	NEW GUIDE TO RATIONAL LIVING *Albert Ellis, Ph.D. & R. Harper, Ph.D.*	3.00
___	PROJECT YOU *A Manual of Rational Assertiveness Training Paris & Casey*	6.00
___	PSYCHO-CYBERNETICS *Maxwell Maltz, M.D.*	5.00
___	SCIENCE OF MIND IN DAILY LIVING *Dr. Donald Curtis*	5.00
___	SECRET OF SECRETS *U. S. Andersen*	6.00
___	SECRET POWER OF THE PYRAMIDS *U. S. Andersen*	5.00
___	STUTTERING AND WHAT YOU CAN DO ABOUT IT *W. Johnson, Ph.D.*	2.50
___	SUCCESS-CYBERNETICS *U. S. Andersen*	6.00
___	10 DAYS TO A GREAT NEW LIFE *William E. Edwards*	3.00
___	THINK AND GROW RICH *Napoleon Hill*	5.00
___	THINK YOUR WAY TO SUCCESS *Dr. Lew Losoncy*	5.00
___	THREE MAGIC WORDS *U. S. Andersen*	5.00
___	TREASURY OF COMFORT *edited by Rabbi Sidney Greenberg*	5.00
___	TREASURY OF THE ART OF LIVING *Sidney S. Greenberg*	5.00
___	YOU ARE NOT THE TARGET *Laura Huxley*	5.00
___	YOUR SUBCONSCIOUS POWER *Charles M. Simmons*	5.00
___	YOUR THOUGHTS CAN CHANGE YOUR LIFE *Dr. Donald Curtis*	5.00

SPORTS

___	BICYCLING FOR FUN AND GOOD HEALTH *Kenneth E. Luther*	2.00
___	BILLIARDS—Pocket • Carom • Three Cushion *Clive Cottingham, Jr.*	3.00
___	CAMPING-OUT 101 Ideas & Activities *Bruno Knobel*	2.00
___	COMPLETE GUIDE TO FISHING *Vlad Evanoff*	2.00
___	HOW TO IMPROVE YOUR RACQUETBALL *Lubarsky Kaufman & Scagnetti*	3.00
___	HOW TO WIN AT POCKET BILLIARDS *Edward D. Knuchell*	5.00
___	JOY OF WALKING *Jack Scagnetti*	3.00
___	LEARNING & TEACHING SOCCER SKILLS *Eric Worthington*	3.00
___	MOTORCYCLING FOR BEGINNERS *I. G. Edmonds*	3.00
___	RACQUETBALL FOR WOMEN *Toni Hudson, Jack Scagnetti & Vince Rondone*	3.00
___	RACQUETBALL MADE EASY *Steve Lubarsky, Rod Delson & Jack Scagnetti*	4.00
___	SECRET OF BOWLING STRIKES *Dawson Taylor*	3.00
___	SECRET OF PERFECT PUTTING *Horton Smith & Dawson Taylor*	3.00
___	SOCCER—The Game & How to Play It *Gary Rosenthal*	3.00
___	STARTING SOCCER *Edward F. Dolan, Jr.*	3.00

TENNIS LOVERS' LIBRARY

___	BEGINNER'S GUIDE TO WINNING TENNIS *Helen Hull Jacobs*	2.00
___	HOW TO BEAT BETTER TENNIS PLAYERS *Loring Fiske*	4.00
___	HOW TO IMPROVE YOUR TENNIS—Style, Strategy & Analysis *C. Wilson*	2.00
___	INSIDE TENNIS—Techniques of Winning *Jim Leighton*	3.00
___	PLAY TENNIS WITH ROSEWALL *Ken Rosewall*	2.00
___	PSYCH YOURSELF TO BETTER TENNIS *Dr. Walter A. Luszki*	2.00
___	TENNIS FOR BEGINNERS, *Dr. H. A. Murray*	2.00
___	TENNIS MADE EASY *Joel Brecheen*	4.00
___	WEEKEND TENNIS—How to Have Fun & Win at the Same Time *Bill Talbert*	3.00
___	WINNING WITH PERCENTAGE TENNIS—Smart Strategy *Jack Lowe*	2.00

WILSHIRE PET LIBRARY

___	DOG OBEDIENCE TRAINING *Gust Kessopulos*	5.00
___	DOG TRAINING MADE EASY & FUN *John W. Kellogg*	4.00
___	HOW TO BRING UP YOUR PET DOG *Kurt Unkelbach*	2.00
___	HOW TO RAISE & TRAIN YOUR PUPPY *Jeff Griffen*	3.00
___	PIGEONS: HOW TO RAISE & TRAIN THEM *William H. Allen, Jr.*	2.00

The books listed above can be obtained from your book dealer or directly from Melvin Powers. When ordering, please remit 50¢ per book postage & handling. Send for our free illustrated catalog of self-improvement books.

Melvin Powers
12015 Sherman Road, No. Hollywood, California 91605